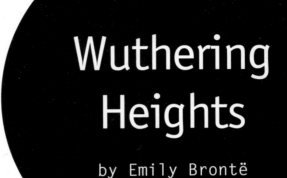

Wuthering Heights

by Emily Brontë

Andrew Green

Series Editors:
Nicola Onyett and Luke McBratney

HODDER
EDUCATION
AN HACHETTE UK COMPANY

The publisher would like to thank the following for permission to reproduce copyright material:

Acknowledgments:

Emily Brontë: from *Wuthering Heights* (1847); **pp. 39, 78, 79, 80: David Punter:** from *The Literature of Terror: A History of Gothic Fiction from 1765 to the Edwardian Age* (Longman, 1996) Copyright 1996 Taylor & Francis. Reproduced by permission of Taylor & Francis Books UK; **p. 27: Virgina Woolf:** from 'Jane Eyre' and 'Wuthering Heights', *The Common Reader* (The Hogarth Press, 1916), reproduced by permission of The Random House Group Ltd.; **pp. 28, 57: Arnold Kettle:** from *An Introduction to the English Novel* (Harper & Brothers, 1951), reproduced by permission of The Random House Group Ltd.; **p. 44: Elaine Showalter:** from *The Female Malady* (Virago Press, 1987) Used with permission of AP Watt at United Agents on behalf of Elaine Showalter; **p. 47: George J. Worth:** from 'Emily Brontë's Mr Lockwood' (*Nineteenth-Century Fiction*, Vol. 12, No. 4, 1958, pp. 315–20); **p. 50: Ellen Moers:** from 'The Female Gothic' (*Literary Women*, 1977), pp. 90–110. By permission of Oxford University Press; **p. 74:** from *The Oxford Companion to English Literature*, 7edn, ed. Dinah Birch (OUP, 2009), p. 856. By permission of Oxford University Press.

Photo credits:

p. 6: © Michael Ochs Archives/Getty Images; **p.24:** © Apic/Getty Images; **p.30:** © Peter Jeffreys/123RF.com; **p.42:** © Photos 12 / Alamy Stock Photo; **p. 46:** © Michal Daniel; **p. 67:** © Eric James / Alamy Stock Photo; **p. 73:** © World History Archive / Alamy Stock Photo; **p. 77:** © Nobby Clark / ArenaPAL/TopFoto

Although every effort has been made to ensure that website addresses are correct at time of going to press, Hodder Education cannot be held responsible for the content of any website mentioned. It is sometimes possible to find a relocated web page by typing in the address of the home page for a website in the URL window of your browser.

Orders: please contact Bookpoint Ltd, 130 Milton Park, Abingdon, Oxon OX14 4SB. Telephone: (44) 01235 827720. Fax: (44) 01235 400454. Lines are open 9.00–17.00, Monday to Saturday, with a 24-hour message answering service. Visit our website at www.hoddereducation.co.uk

First published in 2016 by

Hodder Education

An Hachette UK Company,

Carmelite House, 50 Victoria Embankment

London EC4Y 0DZ

Impression number	5	4	3	2	1
Year		2020	2019	2018	2017	2016

Cover photo (and throughout) © Daniel Kay/Thinkstock

Illustrations by Integra Software Services Pvt. Ltd./Barking Dog

Typeset in 11/13pt Univers LT Std 47 Light Condensed by Integra Software Services Pvt. Ltd., Pondicherry, India

Printed in Italy

A catalogue record for this title is available from the British Library

ISBN 9781471854286

Contents

Using this guide

Why read this guide?

The purposes of this A-level Literature Guide are to enable you to organise your thoughts and responses to the text, deepen your understanding of key features and aspects and help you to address the particular requirements of examination questions and non-exam assessment (NEA) tasks in order to obtain the best possible grade. It will also prove useful to those of you writing an NEA piece on the text as it provides a number of summaries, lists, analyses and references to help with the content and construction of the assignment.

Note that teachers and examiners are seeking above all else evidence of an *informed personal response to the text*. A guide such as this can help you to understand the text, form your own opinions, and suggest areas to think about, but it cannot replace your own ideas and responses as an informed and autonomous reader.

Page references in this guide refer to the Penguin Classics edition of *Wuthering Heights* edited by Pauline Nestor (2003). This edition has excellent introductory material and comprehensive notes.

How to make the most of this guide

You may find it useful to read sections of this guide when you need them, rather than reading it from start to finish. For example, you may find it helpful to read the 'Contexts' section before you start reading the text, or to read the 'Scene summaries and commentaries' section in conjunction with the text – whether to back up your first reading of it at school or college or to help you revise. The sections relating to the Assessment Objectives will be especially useful in the weeks leading up to the exam.

This guide is designed to help you to raise your achievement in your examination response to *Wuthering Heights*. It is intended for you to use throughout your AS/A-level English literature course. It will help you when you are studying the novel for the first time and also during your revision.

The following features have been used throughout this guide to help you focus your understanding of the novel:

Context

Context boxes give contextual information that relates directly to particular aspects of the text.

TASK

Tasks are short and focused. They allow you to engage directly with a particular aspect of the text.

CRITICAL VIEW

Critical view boxes highlight a particular critical viewpoint that is relevant to an aspect of the main text. This allows you to develop the higher-level skills needed to come up with your own interpretation of a text.

Build critical skills

Broaden your thinking about the text by answering the questions in the **Build critical skills** boxes. These help you to consider your own opinions in order to develop your skills of criticism and analysis.

Taking it further ▶

Taking it further boxes suggest and provide further background or illuminating parallels to the text.

Top ten quotation

Top ten quotation

A cross-reference to **Top ten quotations** (see pp. 103–7 of this guide), where each quotation is accompanied by a commentary that shows why it is important.

Introduction

Publication and critical reception

First published in 1847, under the *nom de plume* of Ellis Bell, *Wuthering Heights* is Emily Brontë's only novel. It portrays the powerful and dysfunctional relationships within and between two families – the Earnshaws and the Lintons – and the houses they inhabit – Thrushcross Grange and the eponymous Wuthering Heights. The publication of the novel was controversial. Its frank representation of physical brutality and its overt exploration of sexual passion shocked and affronted many of its earliest readers, and early critical responses demonstrate this. The *Atlas* of 22 January 1848 observes: 'We know nothing in the whole range of our fictitious literature which presents such shocking pictures of the worst forms of humanity.' Response in the USA was, if anything, even more negative. In the February 1848 edition of *Paterson's Magazine* the critic says: 'We rise from the perusal of *Wuthering Heights* as if we had come fresh from a pest-house.' And in its frank and explicit exploration of raw passion, *Wuthering Heights* still retains something of its power to shock for contemporary audiences.

Other initial responses to the novel, however, were more measured. A critic writing in *Douglas Jerrold's Weekly Newspaper* of 15 January 1848 observed:

> *What may be the moral which the author wishes the reader to deduce from his work, it is difficult to say; and we refrain from assigning any, because to speak honestly, we have discovered none but mere glimpses of hidden morals or secondary meanings.*

> *In* Wuthering Heights *the reader is shocked, disgusted, almost sickened by details of cruelty, inhumanity, and the most diabolical hate and vengeance, and anon come passages of powerful testimony to the supreme power of love – even over demons in the human form. The women in the book are of a strange fiendish-angelic nature, tantalising, and terrible, and the men are indescribable out of the book itself.*

Here we see a critic alive to the ambiguity of the novel and open to its power and 'hidden morals'.

The novel's later life

In spite of (or perhaps because of) such reviews, *Wuthering Heights* did enjoy modest success and it gained still greater renown after 1848, owing to Brontë's early death at the age of 30, the increasing popularity of her sisters' novels, and public fascination with the immense concentration of literary talent within this one family. Naturally, speculation about the biographical details of life in the Brontë household was rife, and focus particularly centred on the sisters' relationship with their infamous brother Branwell. Over the years, fascination as to the possible links between fact and fiction in *Wuthering Heights* and in other works by the Brontë sisters has hardly declined. Even by contemporary standards, *Wuthering Heights* remains a work of astonishing and feral passion, but it has lost the moral taint with which it was initially received. In fact, it has become part of the lifeblood of both literary and popular culture, as the many film, radio, theatre and television adaptations of it attest. The novel is in a sense timeless in its focus on human emotion – love, hate, happiness and fear. Unlike other novelists of the Victorian era such as Charles Dickens, Elizabeth Gaskell, Benjamin Disraeli, Anthony Trollope, Wilkie Collins and Charles Kingsley, Brontë does not deeply engage with the great social issues of her day, although these do impinge on the world of the novel; instead she relates more readily with the untamed interior emotional worlds of the Gothic and Romanticism.

The place of *Wuthering Heights* in the literary canon is now assured, in spite of the fact that F.R. Leavis – the founder of the first English Literature degree at Cambridge University in 1919 – would not include it in his survey of the great tradition of the English novel calling it 'a kind of sport'. It has become one of those rare literary works that transcends the boundaries of culture and entrenches itself in the popular imagination. The novel has been regularly adapted for the screen in English, French, Spanish and Japanese versions. Numerous stage versions of the novel (plays, ballets and operas) also exist as a testimony to the enduring influence it has continued to exert on subsequent generations of artists. And then, of course, there is the famous song by Kate Bush …

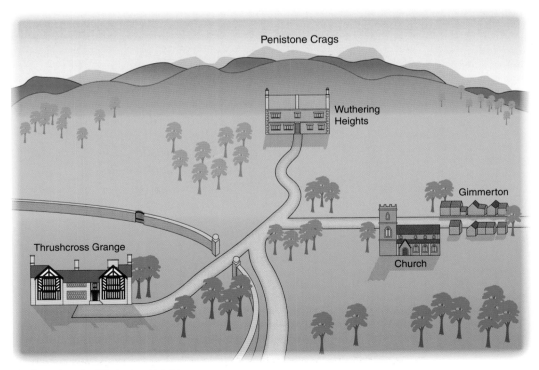

▲ Locations in *Wuthering Heights*

The events of the novel begin in 1801. Mr Lockwood, the first of several narrators, takes up a tenancy at Thrushcross Grange, which he rents from Heathcliff, the unsociable and wild owner of Wuthering Heights. When he pays a visit to Heathcliff at the Heights, Mr Lockwood receives a cold and rude welcome from its inhabitants, whose relationships with one another he fails to understand. He is attacked by the household dogs and attempts to leave, but is forced by bad weather to stay overnight. In his room Mr Lockwood discovers the diary of Cathy Earnshaw, a girl known to Heathcliff in his youth. He falls asleep, but has a terrifying dream of Cathy's ghost appearing at his window, begging to be let in. Heathcliff is awoken by Mr Lockwood's shouts and comes in. When he hears of Cathy's ghost, he asks Mr Lockwood to leave the room. Mr Lockwood then hears Heathcliff sobbing and begging the ghost to enter.

On returning to Thrushcross Grange the next day, Mr Lockwood asks his housekeeper, Nelly Dean, to tell him about Heathcliff, Cathy and Wuthering Heights. Nelly takes us back 30 years to when Mr Earnshaw brought Heathcliff, a waif from the Liverpool streets, to Wuthering Heights. He raised the boy as his own. Cathy and Hindley, Mr Earnshaw's natural children, both initially resent Heathcliff. Out of jealousy, Hindley continues to hate Heathcliff, mentally and physically abusing him, but Cathy and Heathcliff soon become inseparable. When Mr Earnshaw dies, Hindley becomes master of the estate, returning from college with his wife Frances. He forces Heathcliff to work as hired labour, and deliberately demeans and brutalises him. Cathy becomes friends with the Linton family who live at Thrushcross Grange. Her wild manner is somewhat tamed and she is attracted to the refined and gentlemanly Edgar Linton. Heathcliff instantly takes a dislike to Edgar.

Shortly after giving birth to a son (Hareton), Frances dies. Hindley takes to drink, and becomes violent and unpredictable. On one occasion he drops Hareton from the stairs, but the boy is caught by Heathcliff. Cathy agrees to marry Edgar. Nelly knows that Heathcliff will be devastated. Heathcliff overhears Cathy when she explains to Nelly that marrying him would be degrading, and he leaves the Heights before he hears her declaration of love for him: 'I am Heathcliff'. When she learns of Heathcliff's flight, Cathy becomes very ill and is slowly nursed back to health by Edgar, and marries him. The marriage seems happy, but then a mysteriously changed and wealthy Heathcliff returns, determined to have revenge on those he believes have prevented him from being with Cathy. Increasingly a drunkard, Hindley falls into debt with Heathcliff. By the time of his death, Hindley has not repaid these debts, and Heathcliff therefore takes control of the Heights. He vows to raise Hindley's son Hareton with as much neglect as he had suffered at Hindley's hands, so achieving his revenge. Heathcliff is also

Note: Brontë is not consistent in her use of the names Catherine and Cathy throughout the novel. For purposes of clarity, however, throughout this guide, Cathy is used to denote the mother and Catherine the daughter.

determined to ruin Edgar. He elopes with Isabella, Edgar's sister, and this puts him in a position to inherit Thrushcross Grange when Edgar dies.

At first Cathy, pregnant by Edgar, is happy when Heathcliff returns to Yorkshire, but she falls ill after an argument with him about Isabella. A few hours before her death Cathy and Heathcliff are reconciled and reaffirm their love for each other. Cathy has a daughter who she names Catherine, but dies shortly afterwards. Heathcliff becomes bitter, abusive and vengeful, and Isabella leaves him, subsequently giving birth to a son, Linton.

As she is dying, Isabella asks Edgar to raise Linton, but Heathcliff discovers this and takes Linton (a sickly and spoiled child) to the Heights. Heathcliff feels contempt for his weakly son, but loves the idea of him taking control of the Grange. Catherine and Linton, in the company of Nelly Dean and Hareton, meet on the moors. Linton, like his father, treats the illiterate and boorish Hareton with disrespect and contempt. Nelly, who nursed Hareton as a child, is appalled by what Heathcliff has done to him. Catherine, knowing how Heathcliff despises his son, is sorry for Linton. Linton, prompted by Heathcliff, invites Catherine to the Heights. Edgar, however, sensing a trap, refuses to let her go. Reluctantly she obeys her father. When she learns that Linton has fallen ill, however, she hurries to the Heights to see how she can assist. Heathcliff tries to persuade her to marry Linton, whose health is diminishing fast. When this fails, he imprisons her at the Heights and forces them to marry. Soon afterwards, Edgar dies, leaving Linton as master of the Grange, but when Linton also dies, Catherine is left a widow at the Heights, and Heathcliff (as Linton's heir) inherits Thrushcross Grange. We have now reached the point at which the initial narrative started, when Mr Lockwood arrives to become Heathcliff's tenant.

While Mr Lockwood is absent, events come to a climax. Catherine's relationship with her rough, uneducated cousin Hareton flourishes. She teaches him to read and he allows her personality to emerge after the bitterness engendered by Heathcliff's brutal treatment. Confronted by Catherine and Hareton's love, Heathcliff changes almost beyond recognition. He seems to suffer a mental breakdown and begins to see Cathy's ghost and retreats suddenly from the conflicts and brutality of his life. He seemingly withdraws into himself and his fantasy world. He is finally found by Nelly, lying on the bed, stiff with rigor mortis, with the window open and rain pouring in, soaking his body. Only Hareton mourns Heathcliff's death. Heathcliff is buried, according to his wishes, next to Cathy in the graveyard, with Edgar's grave on her opposite side. Mr Lockwood hastily leaves Nelly and on his walk home visits the graves, noting the peacefulness of the spot.

Chapter summaries and commentaries

Target your thinking

- How does Brontë develop her themes, settings and characters as the narrative unfolds? (**AO1**)
- What dramatic methods does Brontë use to shape the reader's responses at crucial points in the novel? (**AO2**)

Volume I

Chapter I

Mr Lockwood has rented Thrushcross Grange from Heathcliff. He is attempting to escape society and an unsuccessful relationship. He recounts a visit to Wuthering Heights, Heathcliff's home. Heathcliff is introduced as an odd mixture of the gypsy and the gentleman, and he arouses ambiguous feelings in Mr Lockwood. His house is, tellingly, a dark and threatening place with fierce dogs and two strange servants, Joseph and Zillah.

Commentary Emily Brontë introduces Mr Lockwood to narrate this chapter. His role in the tale that follows is tangential and only impinges on the terrible and romantic events in certain limited ways. His narrative is what is known as a **frame narrative** – in other words, it is an outer story that contains the main events of the novel. Its intention is to set off and present the main story in the same way as a picture frame is intended to enhance, but not detract from, the picture it surrounds. The reader is introduced to the two central locations of the novel – Thrushcross Grange, which Mr Lockwood rents from Heathcliff, and Wuthering Heights. The chapter establishes an atmosphere of brooding threat and casual violence that characterises the novel.

Chapter II

Mr Lockwood pays a second visit to the Heights. He meets Catherine, whom he assumes to be Mrs Heathcliff. She treats him with suspicion and scorn. When Heathcliff arrives, Mr Lockwood learns Catherine is the widow of Heathcliff's son. There is a violent snowstorm, and Mr Lockwood finds himself unable to return to Thrushcross Grange. At the invitation of Zillah (he is ignored by everyone else) he agrees to stay the night.

Commentary *Wuthering Heights* owes much to the literary traditions of Gothic fiction and Romance. The dark and threatening Heights is similar to the settings for many Gothic novels. Mr Lockwood's confusion as an outsider in the strangely brutal world of the Heights mirrors the reader's own. The strange

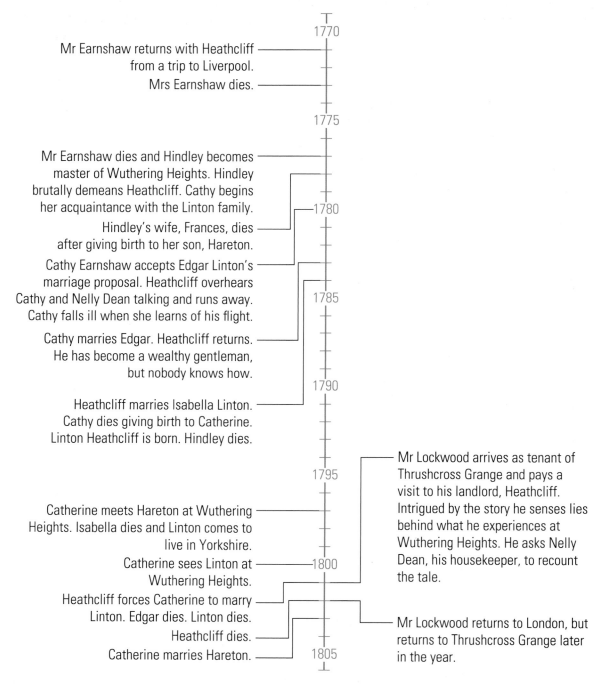

Main narrative · Frame narrative

1770

Mr Earnshaw returns with Heathcliff from a trip to Liverpool.

Mrs Earnshaw dies.

1775

Mr Earnshaw dies and Hindley becomes master of Wuthering Heights. Hindley brutally demeans Heathcliff. Cathy begins her acquaintance with the Linton family.

1780

Hindley's wife, Frances, dies after giving birth to her son, Hareton.

Cathy Earnshaw accepts Edgar Linton's marriage proposal. Heathcliff overhears Cathy and Nelly Dean talking and runs away. Cathy falls ill when she learns of his flight.

1785

Cathy marries Edgar. Heathcliff returns. He has become a wealthy gentleman, but nobody knows how.

1790

Heathcliff marries Isabella Linton. Cathy dies giving birth to Catherine. Linton Heathcliff is born. Hindley dies.

1795

Mr Lockwood arrives as tenant of Thrushcross Grange and pays a visit to his landlord, Heathcliff. Intrigued by the story he senses lies behind what he experiences at Wuthering Heights. He asks Nelly Dean, his housekeeper, to recount the tale.

Catherine meets Hareton at Wuthering Heights. Isabella dies and Linton comes to live in Yorkshire.

Catherine sees Linton at Wuthering Heights.

1800

Heathcliff forces Catherine to marry Linton. Edgar dies. Linton dies.

Heathcliff dies.

Catherine marries Hareton.

1805

Mr Lockwood returns to London, but returns to Thrushcross Grange later in the year.

▲ Timeline of events in *Wuthering Heights*

biblical name of Zillah adds to the sense of threat. The harsh weather of the moors and the blizzard that swoops down to trap Mr Lockwood in the house are used to mirror the harshness of the inhabitants of the Heights and to foreshadow the terrible events that are to follow. This device, particularly favoured among the Romantics, is known as **pathetic fallacy**.

Chapter III

Zillah shows Mr Lockwood to a bedchamber that Heathcliff does not like to be occupied. Mr Lockwood notices the names Catherine Earnshaw, Catherine Linton and Catherine Heathcliff scratched onto the window ledge. He reads Cathy's diary until he falls asleep, only to be haunted by nightmares: the first about a fanatical preacher, the second and more disturbing involving Cathy's ghost. He awakes screaming and Heathcliff enters, evidently disturbed and confused, unaware of Mr Lockwood's presence. Mr Lockwood leaves the room, but not before he sees Heathcliff in floods of tears begging Cathy to come to him. The next morning Heathcliff walks Mr Lockwood back to the Grange.

Commentary Cathy's diary is one of a number of other narrative elements employed by Emily Brontë within the text – including letters from Isabella, Mr Lockwood's journal and oral narratives from other characters. The novel is full of voices, all clamouring to tell their own tales. The various narrative voices of the novel sometimes compete and must be weighed up against each other. The doubling and deliberate confusion of character names (by introducing three Catherines) throws the reader into a state of turmoil, similar to that experienced by Mr Lockwood. This also relates to one of the major concerns of Gothic fiction, which often depends on the fear and confusion that surrounds the repetition of events through the succeeding generations of a family or repeated events (hauntings) in a specific location. Before we have seen Cathy and Heathcliff together and before we know of how they relate to one another, Brontë uses this event to create a connection between them in the reader's mind, and in the context of the supernatural.

Taking it further ▶

Read a variety of extracts from the novels suggested above. How do these authors use multiple narrative perspectives? How does the use of a variety of narrators all involved in the same story affect your perceptions as a reader?

Chapter IV

Mr Lockwood asks his housekeeper Ellen Dean (Nelly) to tell him Heathcliff's story. Nelly explains the complex relationships between the inhabitants of the Heights, explaining that Catherine is the daughter of the late Cathy Linton. She then begins her tale and the time frame of the novel moves back by 30 years (see the Timeline on p. 4). Mr Earnshaw, Cathy's father, returned to the Heights from a visit to Liverpool with Heathcliff, a starving, ragged street-child. Although

Heathcliff was not entirely welcomed by the family, he and Cathy became very close companions. Cathy's brother, Hindley, came particularly to dislike Heathcliff.

CRITICAL VIEW

Heathcliff is often described as 'dark' and a 'gypsy'. Post-colonial critics have been interested in this, and some have gone so far as to suggest he is black. Mr Earnshaw finds him in Liverpool which was a major slave-trading port at the time of the novel. Perhaps Heathcliff is the son of a slave or of mixed race or foreign blood. Old Mr Linton refers to his possible mixed race by describing him as 'a little Lascar, or an American or Spanish castaway'. Whatever the case, Heathcliff is painted as somehow 'other' or alien to the world of the Grange and the Heights. How do you respond to this idea?

Commentary Nelly becomes the third narrative voice of the novel. Note how Brontë establishes the relationships between Heathcliff and Cathy and Heathcliff and Hindley, which will be significant later. The pairing of characters is a significant feature of the novel (see pp. 60–3 of this guide). Through such pairings of characters, Brontë makes her reader think carefully about how characters' situations and behaviours reflect upon and impact upon those around them in the claustrophobic society the novel portrays.

Taking it further ▶

Paired characters in literary texts are often known as doppelgängers. Find out what a doppelgänger is. Where have you encountered doppelgängers in other books that you have read or films that you have seen? How does this relate to Brontë's use of characters in the novel?

WUTHERING HEIGHTS   LAURENCE OLIVIER is Heathcliff and MERLE OBERON plays Cathy in the timeless tale of passion, hatred and revenge, WUTHERING HEIGHTS, a Samuel Goldwyn Company presentation.

THE SAMUEL GOLDWYN COMPANY
© 1989 THE SAMUEL GOLDWYN COMPAN

▲ Heathcliff (Laurence Olivier) and Cathy (Merle Oberon) in the 1939 film version of *Wuthering Heights*

Chapter V

After the death of his wife, Mr Earnshaw becomes increasingly irritable and spoils Heathcliff, his favourite. Hindley's dislike for Heathcliff grows, while the closeness between Heathcliff and Cathy deepens. Cathy demonstrates a manipulative and hard side to her character. Hindley is sent away to college. Eventually Mr Earnshaw dies.

Commentary Here we see the beginnings of the corruption of Heathcliff. It is easy to perceive Heathcliff as a monstrous character, but Brontë's depiction of him is much more subtle. In this chapter, Brontë provides us with an insight into his treatment at the Heights. This seems to provide some reason (if not justification) for the ways in which he goes on to behave towards the other characters in the novel and towards the world in general. His position as an outsider connects him to Mr Lockwood and also, later, to his son Linton. Mistrusted because of his questionable origins and an outsider in the narrow social circle of the Grange and the Heights, he is presented as increasingly and dangerously isolated. Only Cathy likes him, and she and Heathcliff stand together against outside authority. The idea of challenging authority is important in many works of the Gothic canon. Authority, power and abuse are also key ideas in both Marxist and feminist readings of literary works.

Chapter VI

Hindley, the new owner of the Heights, returns from college with his new wife, Frances. He begins to mistreat Heathcliff systematically. Nelly recalls Heathcliff telling her how, for amusement, he and Cathy had spied on the Lintons at Thrushcross Grange. They were caught and Cathy was bitten badly by a dog as they tried to escape. The Lintons, disgusted by the wild manners of the children, drove Heathcliff away. Cathy, however, stayed at the Grange to recover, a visit encouraged and lengthened by Hindley out of his desire to separate her from Heathcliff.

Commentary Heathcliff's voice is now added to the multiplying narrative perspectives of the novel. He is disliked by almost all the inhabitants of the Heights and the Grange, and Brontë uses this chapter to establish firm and close connections between him and Cathy. This is the beginning of a fierce devotion (sometimes represented with literal ferocity) that often manifests itself as the novel progresses. The critic David Punter has commented on how many Gothic works 'do not come out right' because they deal with aspects of life that are untidy, harsh and unacceptable; the disorder and violence of this chapter seem to reflect the disorder and jaggedness of Gothic fiction. Movement between the Grange and the Heights is also important in this chapter, reflecting the constant state of flux within the tale. It is important to remember, however, that these houses are some four miles apart, so they are in many ways distant from one another. This is a useful idea in relation to the two houses, their inhabitants and what they might stand for.

CRITICAL VIEW

A critic writing in *The Examiner* (8 January 1848) wrote of *Wuthering Heights*:

> *This is a strange book. It is not without evidences of considerable power: but, as a whole, it is wild, confused, disjointed, and improbable;*

How useful do you find these ideas in reading the early sections of the novel?

Context

The corruption of childhood innocence is one of the staple themes of Gothic fiction. The rejection of accepted authority and the challenging of social and political taboos are also typical of Gothic fiction, as well as of the Romantic movement more generally.

Liminality: an unfixed position between two opposites – the experience of being on a threshold or a boundary.

Chapter VII

Nelly resumes the narrative. When Cathy returns to the Heights at Christmas, she has been transformed into a lady. She hurts Heathcliff by comparing him to Edgar Linton. In her absence he has been increasingly neglected. The next day, Heathcliff is not allowed to join the children's Christmas party and is banished to his room. Cathy joins him after the party. Heathcliff is determined to avenge himself on Hindley.

Commentary Distance begins to open up in the relationship between Cathy and Heathcliff. Brontë, having established Cathy and Heathcliff as kindred spirits, demonstrates here that there are nevertheless significant ways in which they differ from each other. Social concerns come to the fore as Brontë displays Cathy's dilemma, caught between the desire to be with Heathcliff and the desire to be a lady with Edgar. The concept of **liminality** is important here, as Cathy finds herself in a troublesome place, emotionally torn. The exclusion of Heathcliff from the family party emphasises his position as the outsider. Brontë makes use of such acts of unkindness towards Heathcliff throughout the novel. The injustices he suffers might predispose readers to sympathise with his position and therefore to mitigate his later cruelties.

Build critical skills

Liminality is a key concept in *Wuthering Heights*, which uses opposites to a considerable extent (see 'Dualisms within Gothic', p. 73 of this guide) and which often brings the characters and readers face to face with the boundaries of permissibility. How is this relevant to Cathy's position In Chapter VII and the experiences of other characters in the novel?

Chapter VIII

Hareton, Hindley's son, is born. Frances dies a few months after childbirth. Hindley grows desperate and falls into more and more dissolute ways. The Heights becomes a place of violent confusion. The neighbours stop visiting and

Heathcliff becomes noticeably more savage. Cathy continues to receive visits from Edgar Linton. During one such visit, they have a violent quarrel and Cathy behaves particularly badly and violently to both Edgar and Nelly. Cathy and Edgar reconcile their differences, however, and declare themselves lovers.

Commentary For the first time we see Cathy behaving really badly. This chapter provides a key moment of choice for her – a moment of personal crisis – as she has to choose between Edgar and Heathcliff. Caught between the polar opposites of the refined, mannered, legitimate, included Edgar and the brutal, energetic, illegitimate, excluded Heathcliff, Cathy's choice is established as being between a saint and a devil. This idea is to remain with the reader throughout the novel and culminates in the final image of the characters' three graves – Edgar's within the churchyard, Heathcliff's outside the wall on the wild moorland, and Cathy's straddling the borders between the two.

Chapter IX

Nelly tries to hide Hareton from Hindley, who returns home raging drunk. He catches her and threatens her with a knife, then dangles Hareton over the banisters. Hindley drops the child accidentally, but Heathcliff catches him, thus foiling his own desire for revenge. Later Cathy, unaware that Heathcliff is listening in on their conversation, tells Nelly that she has agreed to marry Edgar. She goes on to say that although she is uncertain about marrying Edgar, she feels that to marry Heathcliff would be degrading. Heathcliff runs away. Cathy becomes very ill after looking for Heathcliff in a violent storm, but he is nowhere to be found. Three years later she marries Edgar Linton. Nelly accompanies her to the Grange and Hareton is left alone with his increasingly brutish father.

> **TASK**
> The hero–villain is one of the stock characters of Gothic fiction. These powerful characters are prepared to use almost any means to gain what they want. They are unashamed of what they do and frequently break the law and reject civilised social values. Yet however evil their actions, they never wholly lose our sympathy. Count Dracula, for instance, remains an attractive and exciting character in spite of his murderous incursions into Victorian society. What other texts have you read or seen where such characters exist? How do the authors make you like these characters in spite of (or perhaps even because of) their unpleasantness?

Commentary This chapter brings to a head the conflict surrounding the triangular relationship between Cathy, Edgar and Heathcliff. The pathetic fallacy of the storm represents the immense turmoil faced by all three characters (but particularly by Cathy and Heathcliff) at this juncture. Heathcliff's maltreatment at the hands of Hindley could find a ready revenge in this chapter, but instead of allowing the innocent Hareton to plunge to his death when Hindley drops him, Heathcliff saves the boy, thus displaying the continuing presence of some humanity in his make-up. Brontë illustrates the intimacy between Cathy and Heathcliff. 'I am Heathcliff', Cathy remarks to Nelly. This is a key moment as we see that Cathy is therefore abandoning her true self in marrying Edgar Linton. Her relationship with Heathcliff is enduring as the rocks, not ephemeral like the leaves of the tree, and as such is an inescapable part of her true nature. On one hand, the distance between Cathy and Heathcliff widens, but on the other it is clear that they are profoundly united.

Chapter X

Heathcliff returns when Cathy and Edgar have been married for almost a year. He is changed: a tall, athletic man, apparently gentlemanly and educated. Cathy is delighted. He stays for tea and she learns that he is lodging at the Heights and winning large sums of money at gambling with Hindley. Heathcliff is a frequent visitor at the Grange and Isabella, much to her brother Edgar's distress, becomes infatuated with him. Cathy, understanding and fearing Heathcliff's motivations, warns Isabella against marrying him.

Commentary The impact of Cathy's choice on Heathcliff is evident. The social world Brontë depicts functions around carefully defined social distinctions — the infamous class system — and it is clear that Cathy's view of him as socially inferior has stung him. If Edgar is acceptable because he is a gentleman, then Heathcliff must become a gentleman himself. The mystery of what Heathcliff does in the three years he is absent from Yorkshire is never answered, but in outward show, at least, the Heathcliff who returns to the Heights is a gentleman. It is not clear whether this is for his own benefit and improvement or to spite Cathy, who rejected him. Heathcliff, for all his surface changes, retains the old lurking brutality in his eyes. Cathy's use of violent natural analogies for his personality demonstrates her awareness and fears.

> ### Build critical skills
>
> Questionable motivations abound in this chapter. Why does Heathcliff woo Isabella? Why does Cathy seek to intervene and prevent the relationship between Heathcliff and Isabella?

Chapter XI

Heathcliff visits the Grange and kisses Isabella. This causes an argument between Cathy and Heathcliff, during which it becomes clear that he is using Isabella as a means of tormenting Cathy. Edgar becomes involved and strikes Heathcliff, who leaves to avoid further trouble. Cathy realises the extent to which she is trapped between Heathcliff and Edgar, and vows to Nelly that she will 'try to break their hearts by breaking my own'. When Edgar enters she throws a faked fit of frenzy.

Commentary Brontë intensifies the emotions surrounding the triangular relationship between Edgar, Cathy and Heathcliff; it grows ever more complex and destructive. Cathy is clearly consumed by emotion: her devotion to Heathcliff and her marriage to Edgar are in direct conflict with each other, and her body becomes a kind of battlefield. Madness is a significant theme in many Gothic texts, and it is significant in *Wuthering Heights* too. In this chapter and elsewhere Cathy's behaviour hovers on the verge of insanity. Her reactions to the situation she faces are self-destructive and all-consuming. Realising that resolution is impossible, she believes that self-annihilation is the only way out. Issues of power come to the fore here as we see a fierce struggle for possession, a struggle that can lead only to destruction as manifested in Cathy's determination 'to break their hearts by breaking my own'. Feminist critics might be interested to explore issues of female weakness and power here. What kinds of power are and are not at Cathy's disposal?

Chapter XII

After three days isolated in her room, Cathy calls for food and water. It becomes evident to Nelly that Cathy is delirious and believes she is back in her room at the Heights. She opens the window and talks to Heathcliff, who she imagines is there. Edgar becomes concerned for her welfare. On her way to fetch the doctor, Nelly rescues Isabella's dog, which she finds hanging by a handkerchief. Later she learns that Isabella and Heathcliff have eloped. Edgar refuses to rescue his sister.

CRITICAL VIEW

The critic for the American magazine *Graham's Lady Magazine* in July 1848 is blunt in his view of the novel:

> *How a human being could have attempted such a book as the present without committing suicide before he had finished a dozen chapters, is a mystery. It is a compound of vulgar depravity and unnatural horrors.*

Commentary In her delirium Cathy seems to revert to her childhood. Freudian readings of the novel might focus on the issue of childhood and childhood fantasy. Think particularly about the respective roles of the 'id', the 'ego' and the 'super-ego' (see p. 82).

Edgar's refusal to save Isabella from Heathcliff effectively condemns her to a life of degradation and violence. Here again issues of gender and power are significant as Brontë explores the relative positions of men and women in marriage and in sibling relationships. We may question whether this is a further sign of Edgar's personal and moral weakness or whether he has in fact warned Isabella sufficiently and she is the creator of her own fate. Whatever we feel about this, Isabella now relates closely to many women in Gothic fiction – helpless and innocent women isolated from all sources of help and left to face the depredations of their tormentors.

Build critical skills

Explain how Brontë uses Cathy's illness to reflect her mental state in this chapter. Why do you believe she wishes to break the hearts of both Edgar and Heathcliff?

Context

It is interesting here to think how Cathy, confined by physical and arguably psychological illness, compares to Mrs Rochester, the psychologically disturbed and abandoned wife of Mr Rochester, in *Jane Eyre* by Brontë's sister Charlotte.

Build critical skills

In Volume I, Chapter III Mr Lockwood is haunted by the ghost of Cathy as a child. How do you feel this is significant in your reading of this chapter?

Taking it further ▶

Remember that although the novel was written in Victorian times, it is set at the end of the eighteenth century. How far, therefore, can it be considered a Victorian novel? Postmodern interpretations would suggest that when an author chooses to locate a text in a time period other than their own, that time becomes part of the author's (and the readers') present. How do you respond to this idea? Think about issues of textual production and textual reception.

epistolary novels: narratives told mostly or even completely in letters. This form allows the author to present their tale from multiple narrative perspectives.

Context

Gothic literature frequently places heroines in positions of emotional extremity. The novel of sentiment or sensibility (as in Austen's *Sense and Sensibility*) was popular in the late eighteenth and early nineteenth centuries. Characters remained morally strong in the face of often extreme trials and frequently displayed extreme emotions. Both of these can be related to Romanticism with its emphasis on individuality and its prioritisation of emotion over reason.

Chapter XIII

Two months pass and it is clear that Cathy will never recover. She is pregnant. Isabella and Heathcliff return to the Heights, but Edgar still refuses to have anything to do with his sister. Isabella sends Nelly a letter describing the isolation, brutality and misery of her existence at the Heights. She bitterly regrets her marriage to Heathcliff.

Commentary In this chapter Isabella carries the narrative forward in a letter. Even though she is living so near to the residents of the Grange, she might as well be on the other side of the world (see 'Isolation', p. 32). A pawn in the game that continues to unfold between Heathcliff, Edgar and Cathy, even the gentle Isabella proves to be capable of violent emotion and indeed physical violence. Brontë, through Isabella's plight, presents us with the vulnerable social position of women.

Brontë uses this chapter to illustrate the true isolation and vulnerability of women. Isabella is totally dependent on her husband and has few rights of her own – in many ways she only exists through her husband, and this puts her in a vulnerable position. Without the help of her brother, she is powerless and can do nothing to rectify the situation. Furthermore, should Edgar and Cathy die childless, Heathcliff as Isabella's husband now stands to inherit Thrushcross Grange (see p. 83).

Context

In the eighteenth century, writers such as Aphra Behn (*Love-Letters Between a Nobleman and His Sister*), Samuel Richardson (*Pamela* and *Clarissa*), Henry Fielding (*Shamela*), Oliver Goldsmith (*The Citizen of the World*) and Tobias Smollett (*The Expedition of Humphry Clinker*) produced immensely popular epistolary novels.

Chapter XIV

Nelly visits Isabella. While at the Heights, she speaks to Heathcliff, telling him not to trouble Cathy any more. He refuses, claiming that Cathy loves him more than she loves her husband. Isabella and Heathcliff express their mutual hatred. Heathcliff asks Nelly to take a letter to Cathy. She agrees as Heathcliff threatens that he will break into the Grange to speak to Cathy in person if she refuses.

Context

Revenge for maltreatment is also a key theme in *King Lear* (see p.76) and an entire sub-genre (Revenge Tragedy) was immensely popular in the Elizabethan and Jacobean theatre. Gothic writers frequently explore the topic of revenge.

Commentary It is clear that Heathcliff has married Isabella out of a vengeful desire to hurt both Cathy and Edgar. A fuller exploration of revenge in *Wuthering Heights* can be found on page 71. He has no sympathy for Isabella; in fact, he despises her because, knowing the kind of man he was and surely knowing how he felt (and continues to feel) about Cathy, she still married him. The combination of passionate love and extreme brutality that Heathcliff embodies makes him an undeniably Romantic figure.

TASK

Byronic heroes rebel against conventional morality, defy fate, are proud, moody, cynical and defiant, are often miserable, scorn their fellow men and are implacable in revenge, yet are also capable of passion and affection. Read up about the Byronic hero at www.wwnorton.com (you can find a full weblink on p. 110). How far do these characteristics seem to relate to Heathcliff?

Volume II

Chapter I

Nelly gives Cathy Heathcliff's letter. Cathy now appears beautiful in an unearthly, almost ghostly way. Heathcliff arrives and their reunion is bittersweet. Their conversation captures the complexities of peace and torment, acceptance and betrayal, love and revenge that characterise their relationship. Cathy knows she is dying and insists that Heathcliff stays. She faints and Heathcliff passes her to Edgar, then leaves to await news.

Taking it further ▶

Read a selection of extracts from the novels suggested or even the whole texts. How do authors use the epistolary form to develop their narratives?

Byronic: Named after the Romantic poet Lord Byron, Byronic heroes are ambiguous heroic figures, even anti-heroes. They are strong, spirited and attractive, but at the same time frequently rebellious and flawed.

Build critical skills

In structural terms, it is interesting to consider why Brontë chose to begin Volume II here rather than after Cathy's death. Why do you think this is the case? What effect does it have on you as a reader?

Commentary This chapter forms a passionate, emotional climax to the relationship between Cathy and Heathcliff. Nelly comments on what a 'strange and fearsome picture' they make. Their love is brutal and animalistic and seems almost like madness (see p. 34). The intensity of the reunion between Cathy and Heathcliff reminds the reader of the storm that broke on the night when Heathcliff ran away. The parallel between these two key moments in the text is important, and this is a structural device that Brontë uses extensively throughout *Wuthering Heights* (see p. 63). In the course of their meeting, Heathcliff in particular appears more like an animal than a man.

> ## TASK
> Imagine you are writing a new screen adaptation of *Wuthering Heights*. Using this chapter or part of it as a stimulus, write the scene. Write an accompanying critical commentary in which you explore the choices you made in representing this scene. Consider:
> - what you opted to put in
> - what you opted to leave out
> - how you set about 'telling the story' using the visual, sound and musical possibilities of the screen medium.
>
> In what ways do you feel screen adaptations add to and in what ways might they take away from the experience of reading a book?

Chapter II

Cathy gives birth to a daughter, Catherine, and dies two hours later. Nelly informs Heathcliff. He curses Cathy and begs her to haunt him so he will not be left without her. A few days after her death, when Edgar is absent, Heathcliff comes to pay his respects to Cathy's body and exchanges a lock of Edgar's hair in her locket with one of his own. Nelly discovers that he has done this and symbolically puts Edgar's hair back along with Heathcliff's. Cathy is buried in a lonely corner of the churchyard.

Commentary Brontë brings the theme of religion to the fore in this chapter (see p. 29). Edgar and Heathcliff hold different views and desires about where Cathy's spirit has gone. Edgar wishes her now to be at peace and envisions her spirit at rest in heaven. Heathcliff, by way of contrast, passionately desires the continuation of his great romance with Cathy. The supernatural is also a significant topic in this chapter (see p. 36). Heathcliff's certainty that Cathy cannot exist peacefully beyond the grave without him is significant. He certainly has no wish to be without her; therefore he wishes her to haunt him in death as she has in life. Recall the scene in Volume I, Chapter III where Heathcliff begs Cathy to come to him after Mr Lockwood has been visited by her ghost.

Build critical skills

Consider Brontë's use of language of the supernatural in Volume II, Chapter II. How does it relate to her use of such language elsewhere in *Wuthering Heights*?

Chapter III

Isabella arrives at the Grange. She has run away from Heathcliff who has reacted extremely violently in his agony over Cathy's death. We learn that he has almost killed Hindley, and has thrown a knife at Isabella when she taunted him. Isabella leaves, never to return to the neighbourhood again. She is pregnant when she leaves Yorkshire and will later give birth to Linton, who will play a significant role in the development of the narrative when Isabella dies 12 years later. Six months after Cathy's death, Hindley dies, and Hareton is left in the care of Heathcliff, who is determined to wreak a posthumous revenge on Hindley by brutalising his son.

Commentary Isabella contributes to the narrative again. Far from bringing an end to conflict, Cathy's death has ignited a new and terrible passion in Heathcliff. His love for Cathy, unlike Edgar's, remains unrequited and unfulfilled, hence his desire that she should continue to haunt him. He takes out his anger on those immediately around him – his wife and Hindley. The events of the past only serve to feed the flames of further cycles of violence and repression, and a further opportunity for this arises when Hindley dies, leaving Heathcliff free to avenge his own maltreatment at Hindley's hands on Hareton. As Laura Kranzler (2000) writes of Elizabeth Gaskell's Gothic tales: 'One of the most chilling fears that informs these stories is the threat of ancestral repetition.' This chapter provides good opportunities to explore the idea of 'ancestral repetition' in *Wuthering Heights* and to consider how useful it is as an idea in developing your reading of the novel.

Chapter IV

Twelve years pass. Catherine grows up, seeming to combine the good qualities of both the Lintons and the Earnshaws. Her father is anxious for her safety and forbids her to leave the park of the Grange on her own. She, however, dreams of exploring further afield. When Isabella falls ill, Edgar at last agrees to see his sister again and undertakes a long journey to visit her. While he is away, Catherine manages to deceive Nelly and goes exploring. Nelly eventually finds her safe at the Heights with her cousin Hareton. Heathcliff is not at home.

Commentary With the passage of the years, the focus of the narrative shifts from the adult generation to the world of their children. It is useful to consider this in relation to ideas of generational repetition and also to consider how and in what ways the narrative voices of the novel shift in order to reflect this change. The contrast is abrupt and harsh, as is so much in this very jagged novel. The events of the second half of the novel can, in many ways, be seen as a reflection or a replaying of the events of the first half, with Catherine taking on the position of Cathy. Catherine's meeting with Hareton – the son of Hindley, who Heathcliff is determined to brutalise – sows the seeds of possibility for a happier future.

> **TASK**
>
> Brontë pairs many characters in this chapter: Nelly and Hindley, Hindley and Heathcliff, Heathcliff and Cathy, Cathy and Isabella, Isabella and Hindley, Hareton and Linton, Heathcliff and Edgar. Take each pairing in turn and explain the effects Brontë achieves by creating each pairing.

> **Build critical skills**
>
> The reader is tempted to see the children's generation as a second chance – will Catherine achieve happiness where her mother failed? Are redemption and resolution possible?

Chapter V

Isabella dies and Edgar returns to the Grange with Linton. That evening, Joseph arrives from the Heights demanding that Linton be sent to Heathcliff, the boy's father.

Commentary Brontë draws a clear parallel between Heathcliff's arrival from Liverpool with Earnshaw and the arrival of Linton with Edgar. Both Heathcliff and Linton come as outsiders, but their personalities are strikingly at odds. Heathcliff's vigour and determination contrast with Linton's frailty and lack of drive. While there was an obvious affinity and connection between Heathcliff and Cathy, it is immediately evident that Catherine and Linton are very different from each other. It is useful to consider how this compares to Cathy's early encounters with Edgar. Heathcliff's almost omniscient power is evident in his knowledge that Linton has arrived at the Grange. Like Isabella, Linton becomes a pawn in the battle between Edgar and Heathcliff.

Chapter VI

The next morning Nelly takes Linton to the Heights. Linton learns for the first time about his father, as Isabella never spoke of him. Heathcliff and Joseph both show contempt for the delicate boy. Heathcliff, however, expresses his intention of looking after Linton. This is motivated not by affection or by a sense of parental duty, but because Linton is the heir to the Grange. Heathcliff wishes the boy to survive at least until Edgar is dead so that he can inherit the estate.

Commentary Father-figures in this novel are almost without exception absent, damaging or inadequate. The novel is full of children who have no good male role models. Linton, too, is in this situation. He arrives at the Heights knowing nothing of his father, as his mother never talked about Heathcliff, and Linton — a frail, inadequate, and in many ways unlikeable young man — finds himself abandoned in a cold and harsh environment. In this we can compare him to several other characters in the novel, particularly Heathcliff, Hindley, Hareton and Catherine. According to Victorian inheritance law, property could not pass down a female line. Catherine, therefore, although she is Edgar's child, cannot inherit the Grange as long as there is a living male relative. Heathcliff knows this, hence his desire for Linton to outlive Edgar. If he does so, the Grange will become Linton's and therefore effectively Heathcliff's.

Chapter VII

Linton proves to be selfish and disagreeable, always complaining about his health. On Catherine's 16th birthday, she and Nelly stray onto Heathcliff's land. He invites them back to the Heights and tells Nelly he wants Catherine to marry Linton. Edgar learns of this visit and forbids Catherine to go there again. She begins a secret correspondence with Linton. Nelly discovers this, burns all the letters, and vows to tell Edgar if it continues.

Taking it further ▶

Although Brontë was a Victorian, she sets her novel at the end of the eighteenth century. Why do you think she elected to do so? How and in what ways should you use Victorian context as a way of understanding the novel?

CRITICAL VIEW

'Children in this novel rarely find protection with their parents.' By exploring examples from the text, explain the extent to which you agree.

TASK

Write a short critical analysis of Brontë's use of liminality and trespass in this chapter.

Commentary The inheritance plotline continues. Heathcliff tries to secure control of the Grange (the gentleman's house) by engineering a marriage between Linton and Catherine. Liminality is a very important concept in this chapter; the characters (especially Catherine) repeatedly cross borders. The idea of trespass, both in its legal sense of going on to another's territory and in its biblical sense of sin, is also important.

Chapter VIII

Edgar is confined to the house by illness. Catherine grows increasingly worried about being left alone when her father dies. Taking a walk with Nelly, Catherine becomes trapped outside the walls of the Grange park (a strange reversal of the images of imprisonment found elsewhere in the novel). Heathcliff finds her there and prompts her to pay another visit to the Heights to see Linton, whom he claims is dying of a broken heart. Nelly agrees to accompany her.

Commentary In this chapter, Brontë adds an interesting twist to the idea of entrapment in that Nelly Dean and Catherine are not locked into a place they do not want to be, but rather locked out of where they do want to be. The wall of the park is another of the novel's many boundaries. It represents safety, whereas the moorland on which Nelly and Catherine find themselves represents threat, as they fall once more under Heathcliff's power. It is useful to consider the different roles of boundaries in the novel. When are they a means of protection? When are they a means of limitation? When are they a source of active danger?

> **TASK**
>
> Characters in *Wuthering Heights* often find themselves either looking out of places they do not wish to be or looking in on places where they do wish to be. Select two or three of these situations. You might want to consider the visitation of Cathy's ghost, Heathcliff's relationship with the family at the Heights and other key episodes. In each case consider the significance of these episodes and compare the effects Brontë achieves through them.

Chapter IX

Linton greets Catherine ungraciously when she arrives. He is full of complaints, but tells Catherine he wants to marry her. They argue about the relationship between husbands and wives in general and as displayed in the relationships between their respective parents. Catherine pushes Linton, making him cough so badly that she feels obliged to promise to return the next day. That night Nelly, who disapproves of going again to the Heights, catches a violent cold and is confined to her room. Catherine uses her evenings while both her father and Nelly are ill to continue her visits to Linton.

Commentary This chapter highlights the binary opposites of imprisonment and freedom. Nelly Dean's confinement to the sick room opens the way for

CRITICAL VIEW

In the Afterword to *Fireworks*, Angela Carter writes about Gothic as a form. She says:

> *Characters and events are exaggerated beyond reality, to become symbols, ideas, passions.*

Select a variety of characters and events from *Wuthering Heights* that you feel are 'exaggerated beyond reality' and explain how useful you find this idea.

Catherine to continue visiting Linton. Neither Linton nor Catherine is really free in their actions. Although Catherine seems to exert her own free will in continuing to visit Linton, she is in fact being manipulated by Heathcliff and is also reacting against Edgar's restrictions. The chapter also deals with issues of love and power and the relationship between them. Binary opposites of this sort are crucial throughout the novel and are a typical feature of Gothic texts. Consider where else you find them in the novel and in your wider reading and consider the uses to which Brontë and/or other authors put them.

Chapter X

Three weeks later, Nelly discovers what has been going on. Catherine recounts her visits to the Heights. Linton appears as a manipulative invalid, prone to temper tantrums. We also hear of her inauspicious meetings with Hareton. Catherine's feelings for Linton are clearly based on sorrow and sympathy, not love. Nelly informs Edgar of Catherine's visits, and he forbids her to continue. He does, however, write to Linton, inviting him to visit the Grange.

Commentary Catherine joins the list of the novel's narrators. We see the stark differences between Catherine and Linton, and Brontë exposes the true basis of their relationship. Although he is in many ways a weak and pathetic character, Linton (like his father) is an artful manipulator. Vulnerability and goodness are often equated with one another, but here Brontë paints a different picture — Linton does not win undivided sympathy. Through Catherine's meetings with both Linton and Hareton, we inevitably draw comparisons between the two men. This is another example of Brontë's structural use of character doubling in the novel. By inviting Linton to the Grange, Edgar is making another move in his ongoing battle against Heathcliff.

> ### Build critical skills
>
> How free are the characters within this novel to act independently, and how far are they at the mercy of forces beyond their control? Explore this idea in relation to a variety of characters.

> ### TASK
>
> Think about the following marriages in the novel. How far are they based on love, and how far are they based on the desire to gain or demonstrate power? Write a short paragraph about each:
> - Cathy and Edgar
> - Catherine and Linton
> - Isabella and Heathcliff
> - Frances and Hindley

Chapter XI

Nelly suggests to Mr Lockwood that he might become interested in Catherine, then returns to her main narrative. Edgar admits to his worry about what will become of Catherine should he die. He writes to Linton, asking to see him, but Heathcliff refuses to allow Linton to visit the Grange. Edgar will not consent to Catherine visiting the Heights, but eventually concedes to a meeting on the moor, with Nelly's supervision. Edgar wishes Catherine to marry Linton so she will not have to leave the Grange when he dies.

Commentary The sudden pulling back to the frame story, as Nelly Dean talks to Mr Lockwood, comes as a surprise. It serves to remind us how complex the narrative structure of the novel actually is. Mr Lockwood's is the surface layer of the narrative, through which we have filtered Nelly Dean's narrative, which itself draws on narrative inputs from a range of the other characters involved in the tale. The reader needs to remain carefully alert to these complex interacting narratives. Catherine's vulnerable position as an unmarried woman is emphasised. Edgar worries about what will become of her when he dies, leaving her unmarried and unprotected. Marriage to Linton, whatever its shortcomings, would at least mean that Catherine will be provided for.

CRITICAL VIEW

John Farrell of the University of Texas writes:

The reader's role in Wuthering Heights, *in the first instance, is to break through the locked and gated narrative that the discourse of Nelly and Lockwood offer.*

What do you make of his view that their discourse is 'locked and gated'? If he is right, what are Mr Lockwood and Nelly seeking to conceal? To what extent are their narratives reliable?

Chapter XII

Nelly and Catherine ride out to meet Linton. They nearly reach the Heights before they find him. He is evidently very ill. He finds conversation difficult, but will not allow Catherine to go, as he is obviously afraid of his father. We strongly suspect that Heathcliff is watching the meeting from some vantage point. Catherine half-heartedly agrees to stay.

Commentary We see the extent of Heathcliff's manipulative cruelty towards Linton. Even when he is so ill, Heathcliff still forces him to go out to meet Catherine, because he desires to extend his power by taking control of the Grange – a feat he evidently goes on to achieve, as we should know by the fact that he was announced in the opening chapter as Mr Lockwood's landlord. By carefully overlaying the narrative elements of her tale Brontë still manages to create the element of suspense and surprise, even though readers in fact already know the outcome. In many ways *Wuthering Heights* is, in this, like a detective story in which the reader already knows (at one level) the outcome of the story. What is of interest is the 'second' story, the act of detection by which we come to an understanding of how these already known events came to pass. The energy, life and power of Heathcliff provide a stark contrast to the pathetic weakness of Linton.

> **Build critical skills**
>
> Both Edgar and Heathcliff control and use their children in pursuing their conflict. Do you think that either man appears morally superior? Explain your reactions.

Chapter XIII

A week later Catherine and Linton meet again. Edgar is much worse and Catherine does not wish to go, but Edgar insists. Catherine, angry at having to leave her father, is disgusted when Linton admits his terror of Heathcliff. Heathcliff appears and asks Nelly how long Edgar is likely to live, as he is worried Linton may die before Edgar. He orders Linton to take Catherine into the Heights and forces Nelly in too. He locks them in, then makes it brutally clear that they will not be allowed out until Catherine and Linton are married. Nelly and Catherine are separated, and Nelly remains imprisoned for five days, unaware of what has happened to Catherine.

Commentary Nelly's and Catherine's enforced stay at the Heights on Heathcliff's orders develops the theme of imprisonment. It also develops the novel's focus on issues of inheritance and the rights of women – Heathcliff knows that if Linton dies before Edgar his hopes of taking over Thrushcross Grange die with him. Heathcliff's total dominance and tyrannical power are evident. All the other characters appear as helpless and vulnerable to his will.

CRITICAL VIEW

In *Gothic: The New Critical Idiom* (1996), Fred Botting writes:

> *Uncertainties about the nature of power, law, society, family and sexuality dominate Gothic fiction … linked to wider threats of disintegration manifested most forcefully in political revolution.*

Such uncertainties typically manifest themselves in literary texts through the use of ruined homes, subversion and disobedience to authority, abuse of power, forced sexual relationships or marriages, and the division of family/societal units. Consider how far such traits are evident at this point in *Wuthering Heights* and elsewhere in the novel.

Chapter XIV

On the fifth day of her captivity, Nelly is released by Zillah. She is allowed to return to the Grange, and Catherine is to follow in time for Edgar's funeral. He is not yet dead, but soon will be. On her return to the Grange, Nelly sends a rescue party to release Catherine, but the men come away without her, fooled by Heathcliff's lies. Early the next morning, however, Catherine returns by herself, having forced Linton to help her escape. Edgar dies peacefully, unaware of Catherine's marriage to Linton.

Commentary Edgar has died before changes can be made to his will to ensure Catherine's future security. This now leaves Catherine effectively at

Heathcliff's mercy. Heathcliff acquires ever greater powers and through his control over Linton, he now effectively has control of Thrushcross Grange. Cathy chose Edgar over Heathcliff because Heathcliff was not a gentleman and because she believed this would degrade her. In a vengeful and painfully ironic narrative reversal Heathcliff, in gaining control of the Heights and the Grange, is now well on the way to becoming the gentleman that he believes he needs to be in order to be acceptable to her (see summary and commentary for Volume I, Chapter IX).

Context

Isolation and imprisonment are common features of Gothic fiction. Ann Radcliffe's heroines in *The Mysteries of Udolpho* and *The Italian* find themselves trapped and helpless in castles, caverns or dark forests. There are scenes of imprisonment in Bram Stoker's *Dracula* and in *The Monk* by Matthew Lewis. Psychological imprisonment is also important – Renfield, in *Dracula*, is incarcerated in an asylum and mentally entrapped by the Count.

Chapter XV

Heathcliff collects Catherine from the Grange to take care of Linton. Now Heathcliff has achieved what he wants, he no longer has any interest in his son. Heathcliff tells Nelly that he asked the sexton to uncover Cathy's coffin so he could see her face again. Dissuaded from this, he struck out the side of her coffin and bribed the sexton to put his body in with Cathy's when he dies. He explains that Cathy's spirit has haunted him night and day since she died. He goes on to tell how, on the night of her burial, he dug up her coffin to embrace her one last time. Ever since then he has felt her by turns comforting and tormenting presence.

Commentary The profundity of Heathcliff's ongoing relationship with Cathy, even after death, is illustrated by Brontë in the grotesque detail of this chapter. Heathcliff envisages both a bodily (though not sexual) and spiritual unity with Cathy. The striking out of the side of the coffin and his desire to be buried right next to her illustrate his desire to be reunited. The dichotomy of comfort and torment sums up the relationship between Heathcliff and Cathy. The continual haunting he describes suggests that Heathcliff may be mad – an interpretation also suggested by his extreme behaviour throughout the novel. The dividing line between sanity and insanity is narrow. This is another of the liminal states of the novel.

Chapter XVI

Nelly's narrative has now almost reached the present. Heathcliff refuses to allow a doctor to be called for Linton. Finally Linton dies leaving everything to Heathcliff in his will, and Catherine is left destitute. One day when Heathcliff is out, Catherine meets Hareton. He feels sorry for her and makes friendly advances. He wishes her to read to him and to teach him to read, as he is illiterate. She refuses harshly.

Commentary As so often in the novel, revenge for wrong is exacted not on the perpetrator, but on an innocent party; here, Hareton suffers at Catherine's hands for Heathcliff's actions. Hareton's conciliatory approach to Catherine, however, is an indication of a break in the storm and offers a potential way out of the cycle of violence and unforgiveness that has developed. It is useful to connect the events of this chapter and the situations of the characters to Brontë's thematic concerns of culture and nature, revenge and violence.

Taking it further ▶▷

For two very different treatments of women's rights of inheritance in the nineteenth century, consider Jane Austen's *Pride and Prejudice* and Wilkie Collins' *No Name*. The former is of interest because it is set roughly contemporaneously with *Wuthering Heights*, the latter because it is another Victorian novel. Other comparisons emerge as *Pride and Prejudice* is a social comedy and *No Name* is a sensation novel. In what ways are the predicaments faced by the Bennet sisters and the Vanstone sisters similar to and different from the problems faced by female characters in *Wuthering Heights*?

Build critical skills

Think about who educates whom in the novel and how they do so. How far and in what ways are knowledge and ignorance used as tools for controlling others in the novel?

Chapter XVII

Mr Lockwood visits the Heights to end his tenancy at the Grange. He gives Catherine a note from Nelly. Hareton tries to take it to Heathcliff but, seeing her upset, does not do so. She cannot reply to the letter as she has no paper and no books to write on. She mocks Hareton, the only possessor of books in the household – Heathcliff uses them to torment him with his ignorance. He fetches the books for Catherine, but then slaps her when she persists in her cruel mockery of him. Mr Lockwood concludes his business with Heathcliff and stays for a meal.

Commentary Books play an important role in the relationship between Hareton and Catherine. Dependency and education are important ideas here, and can be considered more widely in the novel. It is also interesting to look at the relationship between knowledge and ignorance in the novel and how these ideas could be related to Freudian, Marxist and feminist interpretations of the novel with their different emphases on personal development and social power.

Chapter XVIII

It is the autumn of 1802, Mr Lockwood is in the vicinity on a hunting trip and returns to the Grange. He finds that it is almost deserted, and Nelly has moved to the Heights. He goes to the Heights to see what has changed, and finds Catherine teaching Hareton how to read. The lesson is interspersed with kisses and kind words. Nelly is pleased to see Mr Lockwood and tells him how a fortnight after he left the Grange, she was summoned by Heathcliff to the Heights to keep Catherine out of his way. She recounts the ending of the animosity between Catherine and Hareton, hastened by Hareton's injury in a shooting accident.

Commentary The relationship between Hareton and Catherine indicates the hard-won unity of the houses of Earnshaw and Linton, the Heights and the Grange. Heathcliff's relinquishment of power and control begins, and this ushers in a new era. The lessons in reading which Catherine is giving to Hareton are in stark opposition to the policy of brutalisation carried out by Heathcliff, and point the way to a brighter, 'educated' future, as if the ignorance and violence of the past is to be banished. Note how far the kisses and kind words are from the brutal kisses of Heathcliff and Cathy and how far the kind words are from the cursing that characterises the earlier part of the novel. Here we have something far more akin to conventional romance.

Chapter XIX

The next day a conflict arises between Heathcliff and Catherine. Hareton finds himself caught in the middle of his fear of Heathcliff and his love for Catherine. Heathcliff unexpectedly backs out of the confrontation. He is struck by the resemblance between Hareton, Catherine and Cathy. He no longer takes any interest in everyday life, but is totally absorbed with Cathy and his memories. He tells Nelly that he no longer feels part of the living world, as he is so close to that of the dead or the immortal.

Commentary Heathcliff sees and feels Cathy in everything – he is incapable of relating to anything except in the terms of his relationship to her. He seems to be haunted by her memory. We remember Cathy's earlier claim – 'I am Heathcliff'. The physical resemblance between Cathy, Catherine and Hareton that he identifies may be part of this, but may also emanate from the new-found harmony in the putative relationship between the young people. The civilised response of Heathcliff, backing away from instead of inducing confrontation, symbolises a new phase in his spiritual union with Cathy and its impact on the physical world.

▲ Emily Brontë, painted by her brother Branwell Brontë

How do Rousseau's ideas in the context box opposite relate to the major concerns and events of *Wuthering Heights*?

Context

Four key ideas of the French philosopher Jean-Jacques Rousseau were taken up by the Romantics:

- increasing separation of Man from Nature
- increasing unhappiness and loss of virtue
- society imposing restraints on the individual
- humans having an innate sense of justice and virtue that leads to principled action.

Chapter XX

Heathcliff all but stops eating and spends all night out walking. He becomes increasingly disengaged from the real world, and claims to be within sight of his heaven. He expresses the desire to settle his affairs with his lawyer. When Nelly reminds him of the need to think of his soul, he informs her that he has his own heaven, which has nothing to do with the heaven of Christian teaching. He refuses to see a doctor and the next morning is found dead at the open window of his room. He is buried as he requested by the sexton. In the vicinity regular sightings of the ghosts of Cathy and Heathcliff are reported. Catherine and Hareton are to be married and leave the Heights for the Grange. The novel ends with Mr Lockwood's visit to the churchyard, where he sees the three graves of Edgar, Cathy and Heathcliff.

Build critical skills

Sir Walter Scott writes:

> *The marvellous, more than any other attribute of fictitious narrative, loses its effect by being brought much into view. The imagination of the reader is to be excited if possible, without being gratified.*

Do you think that Brontë manages to strike the difficult balance between making her tale scary enough without overusing the supernatural and horror?

Commentary Brontë concludes the novel with a symbolic union (the coming marriage of Catherine and Hareton) and reunion (the burial of Heathcliff, which brings him back to Cathy). Note the final image of the crumbling wilderness of the churchyard, and Heathcliff found dead at the window (particularly significant as we remember the importance of previous scenes at windows). Brontë leaves us with the enduring and pregnant image of Edgar's, Cathy's and Heathcliff's graves, which represent the interplay between the civilised and the uncivilised, the refined and the brutal, the holy and the unholy that have been the intellectual battleground of the novel.

Build critical skills

Windows are liminal spaces – the boundary between the internal and the external. Think back over the various window scenes in the novel. What other boundaries do these scenes suggest?

CRITICAL VIEW

The Freudian critic, Thomas Moser sees the window and door images in *Wuthering Heights* as 'female' symbols and keys and the poker as 'male' symbols. He clearly relates them to male and female genitalia. How do you find this idea useful?

Themes

Target your thinking

- What are the key themes of *Wuthering Heights* and how does Brontë develop them as the narrative unfolds? (**AO1**)
- What narrative methods does Brontë use to illustrate her key themes? (**AO2**)

Major themes

Major themes in ▶
Wuthering Heights

Violence

Violence and brutality permeate every aspect of *Wuthering Heights*. Almost without exception the characters, both male and female, commit acts of brutality and verbal aggression. Violence emerges from a wide range of motivations:

- Love
- Frustration
- Revenge
- Desperation
- Isolation
- Black humour.

Cathy and Heathcliff's relationship is full of violent passions and aggressive rows. Their meetings often appear more animal-like than human. Heathcliff's relationships with Isabella and Catherine are likewise characterised by harshness and cruelty, but lack the element of romantic and spiritual passion that somehow redeems his relationship with Cathy. Isabella's elopement with Heathcliff starts with the hanging of the dog, and ends with a murderous attempt on her life. In trying to protect Hareton from his drunken father, Nelly Dean is forced to 'eat' (p. 46) Hindley's knife, and Catherine's frustration at her imprisonment at the Heights finds vent in vituperative words and physical violence against Hareton and Heathcliff.

CRITICAL VIEW

While emotion was … an important ingredient in sentimental fiction, Gothic took its characters and readers to new extremes of feeling, through the representation of scenes and events well beyond the normal range of experience.

(E.J. Clery, *Women's Gothic*)

Such ubiquitous violence has a profound effect upon the reader. To maintain its power to shock, a steady escalation of brutality is needed. It has an impact, too, upon the mentality of the characters; they seem to develop immunity to the frequent acts of horror they experience and participate in. Their perceptions and sensibilities harden, and they enter into a tacit pact of silence. The prevalence of violence in the dysfunctional Linton and Earnshaw households creates a permanent sense of threat. The failure of conventional communication means that words no longer have the power to heal, but seem only to breed further aggravation, until at last Catherine and Hareton are able to forge a new language of reconciliation and love.

Another major theme of the novel is class conflict. As such, the violence we find throughout the novel may be seen as symbolic of larger societal forces. In this sense, violence not only suggests fragmentation but becomes a strangely unifying force.

Build critical skills

Recall violent episodes such as the hanging of the dog and when Hindley makes Nelly 'eat the knife'. In each case, what is the motivation for violence? How do these episodes affect you as a reader? In what ways are they similar and in what ways different in their impact?

TASK

Virginia Woolf wrote that:

[Emily Brontë] looked out upon a world cleft into gigantic disorder and felt within her the power to unite it in a book. That gigantic ambition is to be felt throughout the novel – a struggle, half thwarted but of superb conviction, to say something through the mouths of her characters which is not merely 'I love' or 'I hate', but 'We, the whole human race …' and 'You, the eternal powers …' the sentence remains unfinished.

How would you complete these sentences? Try to capture what you believe Brontë was trying to say.

Class conflict

Wuthering Heights is set during a period of significant social and industrial development. The beginning of the nineteenth century was a period of rapid change as England and much of Europe made the shift from the agrarian to the industrial, from the rural to the urban. The growth of huge urban industrial centres, particularly in the Midlands and the North of England, led to what the German sociologist Ferdinand Tönnies defined as the move from *Gemeinschaft* – a social order based on individuals and small, largely self-sufficient local communities – to *Gesellschaft* – a society based on large, interdependent communities embodying new capitalist models of production and reception.

[Emily Brontë] looked out upon a world cleft into gigantic disorder and felt within her the power to unite it in a book.

CRITICAL VIEW

Uncertainties about the nature of power, law, society, family and sexuality dominate Gothic fiction … linked to wider threats of disintegration manifested most forcefully in political revolution.

(Fred Botting, *Gothic: The New Critical Idiom*, 1996)

As the nineteenth century progressed, such issues particularly exercised social thinkers like Karl Marx and Friedrich Engels who saw in class-oriented society the institutionalisation of inequity and exploitation. For Marxist critics, social order and conflict are central issues. Kettle expresses the essential material and experiential 'reality' of the world of *Wuthering Heights*:

> *The story of* Wuthering Heights *is concerned not with love in the abstract but with the passions of living people, with property ownership, the attraction of social comforts, the arrangement of marriages, the importance of education, the validity of religion, the relations of rich and poor.*

(Arnold Kettle, An Introduction to the English Novel, 1951: 131)

The name *Earn*shaw might in itself connect to the lower class of that family who must 'earn' rather than inherit their livelihoods.

Terry Eagleton, another Marxist critic also focuses in on issues of class and the divergent lived experiences of the characters. He sees such issues as central to a reading of the novel. The Lintons and the Earnshaws represent the class divide, and the conflict between the two families thus becomes symbolic of wider societal divisions between the landed gentry and the working classes. The name **Earn**shaw might in itself connect to the lower class of that family who must 'earn' rather than inherit their livelihoods. Cathy is seduced by the social cachet of life at Thrushcross Grange and envisions herself as the greatest lady of the neighbourhood. Although never totally comfortable with it, she accepts the bourgeois (middle class) way of life. Heathcliff, on the other hand, rejects it. For Eagleton, Heathcliff represents the anger and revolt of the new mobile social workforce seeking to improve themselves and their lot in life. (Remember, he comes to the Heights from urban industrial Liverpool.) Heathcliff desires: 'the triumph of seeing my descendants fairly lord of their estates! My child hiring their children to till their father's land for wages'. The mystery surrounding Heathcliff's origins, ethnicity and social class make him a threat to the established order. He disturbs the status quo because he has no definable or 'legitimate' place within its system. This raises issues of liberty, power and oppression.

Religion

Religion was central in the Brontë household. Patrick Brunty (who changed the family name to the more exotic Brontë) was parson to the parish of Haworth, and so it is not surprising that religion and religious ideas should play a significant part in *Wuthering Heights*. Language of good and evil (see p. 64) plays a significant role in the novel. Heathcliff, for instance, is often described as a figure of evil, though Nelly Dean is at pains to let us see that he is in some ways also an innocent victim.

Joseph and Zillah, Heathcliff's servants at the Heights, are both given Old Testament biblical names, which may reflect on the brutal and vengeful world of that household. There is also Mr Lockwood's vivid dream in Volume I, Chapter III of a visit with Joseph to hear the fanatical preacher Jabez Branderham speak on the subject of his book 'Seventy Times Seven, and the First of the Seventy-First. A Pious Discourse delivered by the Reverend Jabez Branderham, in the Chapel of Gimmerden Sough'. Mr Lockwood in his dream believes that he, Joseph or Branderham have committed that 'First of the Seventy-First,' and are going to be revealed as sinners and thrown out of the church. Jabez Branderham is often thought to be based on the firebrand Methodist preacher, Jabez Bunting (1779–1858). Thus, we might interpret Lockwood's dream as Brontë satirising Methodism as well as establishing a punitive and restrictive view of religion early in the novel. The church building itself is in disrepair which might reflect the decline of the Church of England. When Mr Lockwood interrupts the sermon to denounce Branderham himself as having committed the unforgivable sin the preacher orders the congregation to punish Mr Lockwood, and they begin to attack him. The sound of Branderham striking the pulpit awakens Mr Lockwood immediately prior to his encounter with the ghost of Cathy, thus suggesting a connection between religion and the supernatural in the reader's mind (see p. 36).

Although religion is a significant part of the novel, we might feel that in many ways the characters have been abandoned by God and left at the mercy of evil forces. The final image of the novel also uses conventional religion and the location of Edgar's, Cathy's and Heathcliff's graves as a means of 'defining' the characters.

Civilisation and wilderness

As we saw when considering the theme of class conflict (p. 28), distinctions between rural and urban, between individual and society are important ideas in the novel. Related to this is the theme of civilisation and wilderness. Brontë creates significant contrasts between 'civilised', controlled nature (for example the churchyard and the park) and the untamed wilderness of the moors.

> **Build critical skills**
>
> One of the uncomfortable contradictions of *Wuthering Heights*, critic Terry Eagleton suggests, is that Heathcliff simultaneously embodies and challenges the social order he wishes to contest. How does this make you think about issues of class conflict in the novel?

> **Build critical skills**
>
> How does Brontë's presentation of the afterlife relate to conventional religious teaching?

TASK

Eco-critical theory invites readers to consider how the natural world is used in literary texts. Jonathan Bate has written of 'the capacity of the writer to restore us to the earth that is our home'. Do you feel that Brontë's treatment of the natural world in *Wuthering Heights* 'restores us to the earth', or does she use it in rather different ways? Write a response to this idea.

▲ The wilderness of the moors

Taking it further ▶

The poet William Blake spoke of what he called 'contraries' such as good and evil, happiness and sadness, or innocence and experience. He saw these states not as the opposite of each other, but rather as part of one another: 'good', 'happiness' and 'innocence' have no meaning without 'evil', 'sadness' and 'experience'. Is the same true of Brontë's use of 'culture' and 'wilderness'?

The conflict between 'civilisation' and 'wilderness' in the novel may be related to the two households of the Heights and the Grange and their inhabitants as follows:

Civilisation	Wilderness
Thrushcross Grange	Wuthering Heights
Mr Lockwood	Heathcliff
The Lintons	The Earnshaws
Refinement	Coarseness
Convention	Revolution
Order	Disorder

The two houses play a symbolic role in defining these contrasting ideas. However, it soon becomes apparent, as the battle for control of the houses between Edgar and Heathcliff develops, that the contrast between the two is not as clear as it may seem at a first glance. Both houses are built deep within the wilderness of the Yorkshire moors, and Brontë uses the beauty, ruggedness and danger of this environment to striking effect.

One of the ways in which she exploits this 'wilderness' is through her employment of the elements. Weather conditions are instrumental in the novel. The name of Wuthering Heights is in itself related to the elements. As Mr Lockwood points out:

> Wuthering Heights is the name of Mr Heathcliff's dwelling, 'Wuthering' being a significant provincial adjective, descriptive of the atmospheric tumult to which its station is exposed in stormy weather.

Top ten quotation

The building itself seems to squat on the landscape, its 'narrow windows … deeply set in the wall, and the corners defended with large jutting stones' as if in defiance of the elements.

Brontë frequently uses the elements to reflect the power and raw, elemental emotion of the tale she tells and of the characters. The power of the natural world and its constituent elements – earth, air, fire and water – provide an apt representation of the characters and their shifting emotions as the novel progresses and the elements often appear to be an externalisation of those emotions and their potential. When Cathy speaks of her feelings about Edgar and Heathcliff, for example, she does so in such terms: Edgar is compared to the passing and 'airy' foliage of a tree which will pass and fall, whereas Heathcliff is likened to the enduring rocks – the earth.

From Greek times onwards a complex system of parallels evolved between the four elements and other corresponding bodily organs, bodily fluids, human temperaments and characteristics. We do not need to go into elaborate detail here, but the idea that the elements symbolise and embody certain characteristics is useful. The following table summarises the major correspondences between the elements, human temperaments and characteristics:

Element	Temperament	Characteristics
Air	Sanguine	Courageous, hopeful, playful, carefree
Fire	Choleric	Ambitious, leader-like, restless, easily angered
Earth	Melancholic	Despondent, quiet, analytical, serious
Water	Phlegmatic	Calm, thoughtful, patient, peaceful

TASK

Gather evidence of occasions in the novel where Brontë uses the four elements. In what ways does she relate the elements to different characteristics and temperaments? Does she always apply the same elements to the same characters? How do you think the elements might relate to different weather conditions?

Taking it further

Read the lyrics to Kate Bush's song 'Wuthering Heights' and watch a video of her performing it. How do the lyrics make use of the elements to reflect Cathy's situation and the events of the novel?

Pathetic fallacy

Landscape and the weather can be used to create atmosphere and emotion. Brontë employs this device extensively in the novel, in particular using storms and the continuously changing moors to reflect events and characters. She also uses elaborate descriptions of the interior of the Heights and of Heathcliff's bedroom to provide us with insight into the nature of his character and the household over which he presides.

Let's think about how Brontë uses the weather and related ideas to create effect in two specific passages. In the first, from 'It was a very dark evening for summer' to '... soot into the kitchen fire' (pp. 84–5), a violent storm erupts. The storm is particularly significant at this point in the novel. It may be taken to represent the separation of Cathy and Heathcliff and the intense emotion this evokes in both of them; to symbolise the personal and spiritual turmoil and upset to which their ambiguous relationship leads; to represent the dislocation and division both within and between the Earnshaw and Linton families; to embody the anger of Heathcliff which is to be unleashed against the inhabitants of the Heights as a result of what has just taken place; to be a symbolic presentation of the madness of the characters — as when Nelly recalls Cathy's reaction to the disappearance of Heathcliff: '... I shall never forget what a scene she acted, when we reached her chamber. It terrified me — I thought she was going mad, and I begged Joseph to run for the doctor' (p. 88).

In the second passage, from 'On a mellow evening in September' to 'Nelly, is that you?' (p. 93), Nelly Dean is out in the garden on the night that Heathcliff returns to Yorkshire. Here Brontë uses the elements to create an ambiguously misleading atmosphere. The pleasant natural description of the early autumn evening is given faintly threatening overtones by the 'undefined shadows' that prefigure Heathcliff as he awaits Nelly's return — a prelude not to autumnal fruitfulness, comfort and pleasure, but rather to fear. Brontë uses the weather to prepare for and to contrast the emotions and atmosphere of Heathcliff's return. The fine weather and the 'soft, sweet air' are soon to be lost in the blast of winter, as the peace of the Heights and the Grange is to be devastated by Heathcliff's anger.

Isolation

Isolation is a central theme in *Wuthering Heights*. Its importance is established in the opening sentences of the novel when Mr Lockwood, on his first arrival in Yorkshire, comments: 'In all England, I do not believe that I could have fixed on a situation so completely removed from the stir of society.'

It is easy to forget in the claustrophobic world of the novel how isolated the locations of the Heights and the Grange are. The Heights is four miles from the Grange, and both houses are some distance from the nearest village — Gimmerton. As such, the Grange and the Heights are somehow cut off from normality and seem to be beyond normal societal expectations and codes.

Within the tight-knit but in many ways dysfunctional Linton and Earnshaw family circles, people easily fall into disfavour or are alienated from their families and neighbours. Although they are forever surrounded by the members of their family, many of the characters suffer an increasing sense of loss and loneliness, unable as they are to develop meaningful, loving and trusting relationships. Cathy and Heathcliff resort to dreams in order to conduct their relationship, and Isabella deludes herself with the fantasy that Heathcliff is some kind of Byronic romantic hero. In both cases, any hope of a conventional 'dream' relationship is quickly dispelled.

Almost without exception, the inhabitants of the Heights and the Grange find themselves at one time or another in isolated situations – literally, relationally, morally or psychologically. Such isolation brings with it insecurity. All of the characters (even Heathcliff) display a desperate need for meaningful and reliable companionship. The love and devotion that many of the characters feel for Nelly Dean, in the absence of any lasting maternal figure, is clear evidence of the basic human need for affection and care. The various marriages of the book are proof of a continued yearning for fulfilment and unity; however, with the final exception of the union between Catherine and Hareton, they are not about companionship so much as control, vengeance and confrontation; these marriages prove not to be sources of comfort and kindness but of further pain and brutality. Even the final supernatural reunion of Cathy and Heathcliff does not bring peace, but only further 'haunting'. The novel explores the psychological and social impact of isolation and cruelty, looking at how it can affect individuals, families and the local community.

Taking it further ▶

The French sociologist Émile Durkheim coined the term anomie. This is defined by the Encyclopaedia Britannica as 'a condition of instability resulting from a breakdown of standards and values or from a lack of purpose or ideals'. According to Durkheim such a state typically leads to a sense of futility, lack of purpose, emotional emptiness and despair. The American sociologist Robert K. Merton found that anomie tended to be most prevalent in people who do not have legitimate means of fulfilling their personal goals.

In what ways might these ideas be useful in your reading of *Wuthering Heights*?

As we might expect, in such a closed and in many ways inhospitable community, outsiders are treated with suspicion. When Mr Lockwood first speaks to Nelly Dean she tells him in no uncertain terms:

> 'We don't in general take to foreigners here, Mr Lockwood, unless they take to us first.'

Top ten quotation

She is speaking about Hindley's wife, Frances, but her remarks apply equally well to other outsiders such as Heathcliff, Linton and Mr Lockwood. Perhaps the greatest outsider, however, is Heathcliff – 'that strange … American or Spanish

> **TASK**
> Alienation and authority are key elements of Marxist literary theory (see p. 82). Think in detail about how Brontë approaches these issues in *Wuthering Heights*. How, for example, does she deal with issues of characters' isolation and the psychological impact of being separated from others or of living in lonely places? Who exerts power over whom, and in what ways do they exercise their power?

As we might expect, in such a closed and in many ways inhospitable community, outsiders are treated with suspicion.

castaway' as Mr Linton refers to him. Catherine towards the end of the novel sums up Heathcliff's situation in taunting yet pathetic terms:

> 'Mr Heathcliff, you have nobody to love you … You *are* miserable, are you not? Lonely, like the devil, and envious like him? *Nobody* loves you – *nobody* will cry for you when you die. I wouldn't be you!'

Madness

The boundary between sanity and insanity is often difficult to define. This is certainly the case in *Wuthering Heights* which frequently explores liminal states. Questions of sanity and insanity are often significant in feminist readings of Victorian literature. Gilbert and Gubar's classic work of feminist criticism, *The Madwoman in the Attic: The Woman Writer and the Nineteenth-Century Literary Imagination*, critiques Victorian perceptions and representations of women and womanhood, and considers the ways in which deviation from expected 'norms' was often explained as a form of insanity.

Taking it further ▶

Read one or more of these classic representations of supposed female 'madness' and the abuses it could lead to: Wilkie Collins' sensation novel *The Woman in White*; Mary Elizabeth Braddon's *Lady Audley's Secret*; Charlotte Brontë's *Jane Eyre*; Charlotte Gilman Perkins' short story 'The Yellow Wallpaper'.

Much of what the reader encounters in the novel seems to border on the insane. Heathcliff and Cathy's intensely passionate relationship is a good example, depending as it does on the desire to possess and the desire to punish in almost equal measure. In the words of the cliché, they can't live with each other and they can't live without each other. The nature of their relationship in one sense stays the same throughout the novel, but both characters change in the light of their experiences, and it is the gap that opens up between their desire and their reality that leads both near to if not actually into madness. Cathy recognises this when she observes in Volume I, Chapter XII: 'I wish I were a girl again, half savage and hardy, and free … and laughing at injuries, not maddening under them.' The increasing impossibility of a relationship with Heathcliff and the 'maddening' she expresses here are far removed from the feigned 'frenzy' she affects when trying to get her own way with Edgar and Nelly Dean. (See also analysis of Cathy's character, p. 42.)

Context

Feigned and actual madness plays an important role in a number of Shakespeare's plays: most particularly consider Lady Macbeth (*Macbeth*), Poor Tom and Lear (*King Lear*) and Hamlet (*Hamlet*). You could read these plays if you are not already familiar with them and consider how Brontë's use of madness relates to them as a context.

Heathcliff's excessive and obsessive behaviour also approaches mania. The intensity of his relationship with Cathy and his relentless determination to prove himself manifest themselves in violence, introversion and immense physical and mental drive. He appears to the people around him as a man possessed. The over-riding influence on his life, however, is Cathy. When Mr Lockwood has been visited by the ghost of Cathy and tells Heathcliff of it we see his desperate desire to be reconnected with her, and in Volume II, Chapter XIX he tells Nelly:

> 'I cannot look down to this floor, but her features are shaped on the flags! In every cloud, in every tree filling the air at night, and caught by glimpses in every object by day ... my own features mock me with a resemblance. The entire world is a dreadful collection of memoranda that she did exist, and that I have lost her.'

Heathcliff's extraordinary capacity for brutality, his heightened emotional responses and his iron determination to assert his will no matter what the cost to anyone else seem to be a kind of monomania.

Madness can, in one sense, be seen as the assertion of an alternative and socially unacceptable subjectivity. It is the divergence from what is generally considered 'acceptable' that leads to its being labelled as insanity. Julia Kristeva illuminates this idea when, in *Powers of Horrors*, she argues that '"proper"' subjectivity and sociality require the expulsion of the improper, the unclean and the disorderly'. The problem is, of course, that in pathologising the 'improper', society denies the legitimacy of alternative views and thus risks creating potentially dangerous marginalisation. It is these 'margins' and border subjectivities that many Gothic and Romantic literary works (including *Wuthering Heights*) explore to such great effect.

CRITICAL VIEW

In *Love and Death in the American Novel* (1960) Leslie Fiedler suggests that the whole canon of Gothic literature is in a way a form of madness, comparing it to a 'pathology':

> Some would say that the whole tradition of the Gothic is a pathological symptom rather than a proper literary movement, a reversion to the childish game of scaring oneself in the dark, or a plunge into sadist fantasy, masturbatory horror.

What do you feel about this view with its darkly sexual overtones? How do you think it relates to *Wuthering Heights*?

Several other characters also make seemingly insane choices. Isabella, for instance, persists in her headstrong determination to marry Heathcliff in spite of Cathy's blunt warnings about his true nature and in the face of Edgar's fierce opposition and subsequent rejection. Similarly, later in the novel, Catherine goes against Edgar's edict that she stay at home and takes advantage of Nelly's illness to visit Linton at the Heights, thus placing herself under Heathcliff's power. Such apparently self-destructive actions and the frenzied violence and mindless brutality so common in the novel create a 'mad' world of inverted values.

TASK

Collect a range of examples of Brontë's language that relate to sanity and insanity.

Threats of death and murder are to be found throughout the novel; they are part and parcel of life at the Heights.

TASK

Collect details about the characters who die in the course of the novel. How do they die and what does Brontë use each death to suggest?

Mr Lockwood experiences the 'madness' of his dreams of Jabez Branderham and his haunting by the ghost of Cathy.

Death

Death is never far off in the novel. Cathy, Frances, Isabella and Linton all die young, and Heathcliff (as Mr Lockwood points out) is still very fit and healthy up until his death. Surprisingly nobody dies as a result of the ubiquitous physical violence we see, even where it takes deadly forms. Threats of death and murder are to be found throughout the novel; they are part and parcel of life at the Heights.

Through his violence and his relentless pursuit of revenge, Heathcliff unleashes a deadly threat on the world. Human existence is fragile in Brontë's fictional world. Moral and spiritual destruction constantly threaten to engulf the novel. The ubiquity of violence and annihilation illustrate a deadly moral vacuum. Consider here Durkheim's concept of anomie (see p. 33).

Life and death are closely intertwined in *Wuthering Heights*. When Cathy dies, Heathcliff laments: 'I *cannot* live without my life! I *cannot* live without my soul!' Her death condemns him to continue living alone, but he sees that his existence from this point on will be living death. This situation is inverted when he himself dies and he and Cathy return to haunt the neighbourhood of the moors in a form of deathly life.

The powerful final image of the graveyard and specifically the three graves of Cathy, Edgar and Heathcliff emphasises the significance of death within the novel. At the same time, however, it strangely undermines the power of death. Death in this novel is not always an inevitable or binding force. Many of the characters survive deadly situations, and Cathy has 'walked' for 18 years, during which she has continued to visit and torment Heathcliff. After Heathcliff's death it is clear that the reunited couple begin a new life.

The supernatural

Brontë makes use of the supernatural throughout the novel, but her use of the device is unconventional. Heathcliff is not supernatural in the sense that he is paranormal; instead, he appears superhuman. He is immensely strong, frighteningly driven, almost omniscient and omnipresent – in every way larger than the world around him. The horror and brutality of his actions make him seem supernatural, but the fearsome power he holds comes from his flesh-and-blood reality. He is capable of feelings and emotions, of bleeding and dying like those around him. The cruel neglect and maltreatment he suffers at the hands of Hindley after the death of old Mr Earnshaw, his protector, show that he is susceptible to natural human responses and emotions, and we have sympathy for him. It is in terms of the supernatural, however, that others seek to make sense of him – he is referred to as a 'vampire' and a 'goblin', and Linton perceives his father as a malevolent spirit looking down from the Heights. At times he appears unnatural in his pursuit of insatiable, passionate and extraordinarily violent revenge, and at others he displays a preternatural awareness of events. He also conceives of himself in such terms. When he speaks of his influence over Linton, he depicts himself as a fearful spiritual presence watching over the boy. A similar effect is created when Catherine and Nelly ride out to meet Linton, when Heathcliff is an over-watching presence, driving them towards wedlock.

The supernatural plays a significant role in the lives of Cathy and Heathcliff. This is foreshadowed by the visitation of Cathy's ghost in Mr Lockwood's nightmare. Cathy also recalls how, as children, she and Heathcliff used to call up the ghosts in the graveyard of Gimmerton Kirk. This prepares the way for Heathcliff digging up Cathy's grave, and for the later sightings of the reunited spirits of Heathcliff and Cathy. Furthermore, it links Heathcliff and Cathy firmly to the supernatural; it is as if the natural world is not sufficient to contain their passion. After Cathy's death this continues; Heathcliff is so aware of the supernatural that he almost becomes supernatural himself. The natural relationship between Cathy and Heathcliff can only take place in the terms of (and actually in) the supernatural world.

The visitations of the ghosts of Cathy and Heathcliff in the course of the novel represent a more conventional deployment of the supernatural.

> ## TASK
>
> Sir Walter Scott writes of the use of the supernatural in fiction:
>
> *… the supernatural in fictitious composition requires to be managed with considerable delicacy, as criticism begins to be more on the alert. The interest which it excites is indeed a powerful spring; but it is one which is peculiarly subject to be exhausted by coarse handling and repeated pressure … The marvellous, more than any other attribute of fictitious narrative, loses its effect by being brought much into view.*
>
> (Walter Scott, 'On the Supernatural in Fictitious Compositions', 1827)
>
> Do you think that Emily Brontë makes effective use of the supernatural, or does it ultimately lose its power because of excess?

Superstition and the supernatural also appear in other contexts. Nelly Dean, out walking one day, encounters an apparition of Hindley as a child: 'as fresh as reality, it appeared that I beheld my early playmate seated on the withered turf'. She takes this 'visitation as a superstitious prompting that she should visit the Heights.

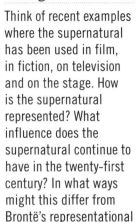

Taking it further ▶

Think of recent examples where the supernatural has been used in film, in fiction, on television and on the stage. How is the supernatural represented? What influence does the supernatural continue to have in the twenty-first century? In what ways might this differ from Brontë's representational methods and times?

Build critical skills

F.R. Leavis excluded *Wuthering Heights* from his classic survey of the English novel, *The Great Tradition*, saying it was a 'sport', in that it had no meaningful connection to the fiction which preceded it, or influence on the fiction which followed it. In the light of your own wider reading, how do you respond to this point of view?

Entrapment

Entrapment and imprisonment are important ideas within the novel. Sometimes this entrapment is literal. Thrushcross Grange, for example, is encircled by a wall beyond which Catherine is forbidden to pass by Edgar. Mr Lockwood is imprisoned within his bed at the Heights when he has his dream of Jabez Branderham and when he is haunted by Cathy's ghost. Cathy is imprisoned in her grave until she is reunited in death with Heathcliff and she also imprisons herself in her room after her violent outbreak against Edgar. Later in the novel Nelly and Catherine are imprisoned at Wuthering Heights before Heathcliff forces Catherine to marry Linton.

CRITICAL VIEW

In 'Repression and Sublimation of Nature in *Wuthering Heights*', Margaret Homans offers a psychological reading of the novel's repeated images of confinement through which:

> *the reader becomes accustomed to Emily Brontë's habitual use of the image of the house, with its windows and doors, variously locked or open, as a figure for varying psychic conditions.*

How helpful is this idea to your understanding of the novel?

On other occasions, however, the entrapment is relational or mental. Nelly Dean is imprisoned by her divided loyalties to almost all of the other characters; as a central presence in all of their lives and all of their 'stories' she finds herself pulled in many directions and able to escape none of them. In the brutal world of the novel all of the characters find themselves imprisoned within the cycle of violence and revenge. It is not until Heathcliff dies, allowing Catherine's and Hareton's relationship to flourish, that this pattern can be broken. Cathy is imprisoned both within her marriage to Edgar and within her mutually destructive relationship with Heathcliff; this is symbolised when she sees herself as imprisoned in her own body, which she refers to as 'this shattered prison' (p. 162).

TASK

Luce Irigaray, in *Passions élémentaires* (1982), offers a feminist credo for the role and the sanctity of the individual within healthy loving relationships:

> *… love is the movement of becoming that allows the one and the other to grow. For such love to exist, each one must keep its body autonomous. One must not be the source of the other, nor the other of the one.*

Consider the relationship between Cathy and Heathcliff, and any of the other marriages in the novel. In what ways do they reflect or diverge from this view of healthy relationships? How does this contribute to your reading of *Wuthering Heights*?

Target your thinking

- How does Brontë develop her characters as the narrative unfolds? (**AO1**)
- What methods does Brontë use to shape the reader's responses to the characters? (**AO2**)

Heathcliff

Heathcliff dominates the novel. He is a man of a thousand contradictions: a beast, a victim, cruel, capable of the deepest love, a baby, a child, a man, heartless, hateful, affectionate, confident, in need of reassurance, a gentleman, sub-human, superhuman, a Byronic hero, a Machiavellian villain, vengeful and forgiving. Readers' perceptions of him shift continually, and no simple summary of him is possible; however, broadly speaking, our sorrow for him at the beginning becomes dislike as the novel progresses, and returns to sympathy as the novel concludes.

Heathcliff dominates the novel. He is a man of a thousand contradictions:

Build critical skills

Compare and contrast Lawrence Olivier's portrayal of Heathcliff in the 1939 film adaptation directed by William Wyler with the portrayal by Ralph Fiennes in the 1992 version directed by Peter Kosminsky. How effectively do you feel they illustrate the complexities of his character?

He is an unprincipled and tyrannical villain. An awe-inspiring man, he evokes absolute fear in most of the other characters. Adept at manipulating the fate of those around him, he turns their lives and property to his own purposes and takes villainous glee in the pain he inflicts. He works to master his own fate – especially his long-desired reunion with his beloved Cathy. He has the dash, fire, mystery and complex attraction of the Byronic hero. We never quite understand him. What are his true roots? Where did he go and what did he do during his absence from the neighbourhood of the Heights and the Grange? We also sympathise with him; an outsider from the moment he arrives in Yorkshire, he is never accepted and is frequently maltreated by those who should care for him. Forever reminded of his dubious birth, background and social status, he is forced into a corner where he has no choice but to defend himself ferociously. Heathcliff is a victim as well as a villain.

On their first acquaintance, Mr Lockwood does not know what to make of Heathcliff. He is a man of uncertain, unacceptable parentage and a social misfit. To Mr Lockwood he appears 'under-bred' and contradictory – a gypsy-gentleman, providing 'a singular contrast to his abode'. The same ambiguity is felt by Nelly Dean when Heathcliff returns to Thrushcross Grange after three years' absence. He has changed and come into unexplained wealth. Uncertainty and mystery multiplies. Nobody knows where he has been and he is now a fine, handsome figure of a man, superior in many ways to Mr Linton. However, he retains his passion, brutality and fire. His eyes tell the tale, and he has become a fearsome and powerful force. Nelly comments on his 'half-civilised ferocity' and his manner, which is dignified but 'too stern for grace'. Her doubts are evident, however, when she ironically informs Cathy: 'He is reformed in every respect apparently – quite a Christian – offering the right hand of fellowship to his enemies all round!' Her use of the word 'apparently' tells a tale. She cannot rid her mind of the younger Heathcliff who she at one point describes as 'possessed of something diabolical'. Isabella strikes a similar note when she asks:

Top ten quotation

'Is Mr Heathcliff a man? If so, is he mad? And if not, is he a devil?'

Taking it further ▶

'Is he a ghoul or a vampire?' I mused. I had read of such hideous incarnate demons.

As Heathcliff is on the point of death, Nelly Dean reflects on his nature, questioning whether he is even human. Read Bram Stoker's classic vampire novel *Dracula* and John Polidori's tale 'The Vampyre' for other examples of the vampire in nineteenth-century literature.

There is no doubt that Heathcliff is an immensely brutish man. He is frequently compared to wild creatures (serpents, lions and wolves) as well as to devils and other supernatural beings. Cathy captures this perfectly. When Isabella is thinking of marrying him, Cathy pleads with Nelly to make Isabella aware:

> 'Tell her what Heathcliff is – an unreclaimed creature, without refinement – without cultivation; an arid wilderness of furze and whinstone.'

Top ten quotation

Shortly afterwards she says he is 'a fierce, pitiless, wolfish man' and Isabella also uses animal imagery to capture Heathcliff's wild and fearsome nature:

> 'I assure you, a tiger, or a venomous serpent could not rouse terror in me equal to that which he wakens.'

Top ten quotation

Edgar Linton tells Heathcliff to his face that his 'presence is a moral poison that would contaminate the most virtuous' and Isabella, who has foolishly ignored Cathy's advice not to marry Heathcliff, says to Nelly, 'Don't put faith in a single word he speaks. He's a lying fiend, a monster and not a human being!' Even after death, Heathcliff appears as a formidable and potent force:

> I tried to close his eyes – to extinguish, if possible, that frightful, life-like gaze of exultation, before anyone else beheld it. They would not shut – they seemed to sneer at my attempts, and his parted lips, and sharp, white teeth sneered too!

Top ten quotation

However, like Nelly, we can never quite forget the personal rejection and brutality with which Heathcliff was treated by Hindley – enough, Nelly opines, 'to make a fiend of a saint'. She sums up her views concisely in the following passage:

> His abode at the Heights was an oppression past explaining. I felt that God had forsaken the stray sheep there to its own wicked wanderings, and an evil beast prowled between it and the fold, waiting his time to spring and destroy.

She also watches his deep sadness and loneliness and observes that he has 'a heart and nerves the same as your brother men!' Nelly is sympathetic. She understands Heathcliff is at war with himself and the world. He is vulnerable and susceptible to normal human emotions.

Build critical skills

How far do you think Heathcliff is presented as a sadist (one who enjoys inflicting pain on others) or a masochist (one who enjoys having pain inflicted upon himself)? Explain your response.

TASK

Using the information about Heathcliff and other ideas of your own, write a one-page summary of your own view of Heathcliff's character.

Cathy is an emotionally volatile and deeply troubled character.

Taking it further ▶

Read the Parable of the Lost Sheep (Matthew 18: 12–14 and/or Luke 15: 3–7); also Jesus' warning against wolves in sheep's clothing in Matthew 7: 15. What do these passages add to your understanding of Heathcliff's character at this point and in the novel more generally?

Cathy

Our first encounter with Cathy is in ghostly form as she haunts a restless Mr Lockwood at Wuthering Heights. This encounter captures the disturbed and pathetic essence of Cathy's nature. When we see her in the flesh she is, from the first, a passionate and often self-centred person. This manifests itself in restless energy and high emotions. Nelly Dean tells us:

> Her spirits were always at high-water mark, her tongue always going – singing, laughing and plaguing everybody who would not do the same. A wild, wick slip she was – but, she had the bonniest eye, and the sweetest smile.

She is deeply selfish, always desiring attention. Wild and wicked with a cruel streak, she manipulates others and is often mischievous and annoying to others. She cashes in on her smile and her beauty, however. When she is obliged to stay with the Lintons after she and Heathcliff have been caught spying on the inhabitants of the Grange we see Cathy's capacity for deception. She acts the part of the lady with her hosts, but when she is at the Heights she has 'small inclination to practise politeness' and Nelly describes her as having 'an unruly nature'.

▲ Kaya Scodelario as Cathy in the 2011 film version of Wuthering Heights

Taking it further ▶▷

Read about *Wuthering Heights* in Gilbert and Gubar's classic work of feminist theory *The Madwoman in the Attic: The Woman Writer and the Nineteenth-Century Literary Imagination* (1979), which explores the characters of Cathy and Heathcliff in detail.

Build critical skills

Gilbert and Gubar are interested in Emily Brontë's use of names. They particularly explore the writing of Cathy's name in its various manifestations (Earnshaw, Heathcliff, Linton) on the windowsill at the Heights. They suggest this reveals a crucial lack of identity which they see as the common lot of women in a patriarchal society: 'what Catherine, or any girl must learn is that she does not know her own name, and therefore cannot know who she is or whom she is destined to be'. How helpful is this idea in considering Cathy's character or other female characterisations in the novel?

Together these characteristics prepare us for the manipulation we see Cathy use later in the novel. In many ways Cathy has a vengeful and controlling nature. She manipulates both Edgar and Nelly, and is unstable almost to the point of insanity. She is also a dangerous woman to cross. She asks Nelly to pass on a warning to Edgar: 'remind him of my passionate temper, verging, when kindled, on frenzy' and at the same time reprimands Nelly for being insufficiently caring: 'I wish you could dismiss that apathy out of your countenance, and look rather more anxious about me!' On one occasion she takes her threat so far as to have what Nelly calls 'one of her senseless wicked rages', 'dashing her head against the arm of the sofa, and grinding her teeth, so that you might fancy she would crash them to splinters!' Cathy will go to any lengths to manipulate those around her. Her frenzy makes us question her sanity especially when we read how she 'increased her feverish bewilderment to madness, and tore the pillow with her teeth'. Readers may question whether Cathy's madness is affected or genuine. Many things in the novel border on the insane. Cathy's behaviour reflects this. Her fire and passion become, at times, something almost other-worldly. Just before Cathy's death at the beginning of Volume II, Nelly comments on her 'unearthly beauty', as if she is already transforming into some kind of supernatural being, and her sudden, often violent emotional shifts show that she is no longer part of the rational world.

TASK

Elaine Showalter, a feminist critic and theorist, writes about women and sexual desire. In this passage she is writing specifically about Bertha Mason, the insane wife of Mr Rochester in Charlotte Brontë's novel *Jane Eyre*:

As Rochester tells the story […] after their marriage, Bertha becomes 'intemperate and unchaste', a monster of sexual appetite who finally is pronounced mad by 'medical men'. Brontë's account echoes the beliefs of Victorian psychiatry about the transmission of madness: […] the reproductive system was the sources of mental illness in women […] and is linked to the periodicity of the menstrual cycle […] Bertha suffers from the 'moral insanity' associated with women's sexual desires.

Look closely at Emily Brontë's representation of Cathy and Isabella. Write a few paragraphs exploring how Showalter's ideas might apply to *Wuthering Heights* and the idea of female 'madness'.

She is the one character who has the capacity to control Heathcliff. Brontë demonstrates throughout the novel the extent to which they are kindred spirits. Their relationship, however, is evidently self-destructive. It operates at such a passionately intense level that the two characters are in many ways inseparable. This is probably nowhere better captured than in the scene where Cathy discusses her choice to marry Edgar. Her sense of her position in society conflicts with Heathcliff's social unacceptability. At the same time, however, she cannot escape the intimate bond that exists between her and Heathcliff:

'It would degrade me to marry Heathcliff now; so he shall never know how I love him: and that, not because he's handsome, Nelly, but because he's more myself than I am. Whatever our souls are made of, his and mine are the same; and Linton's is as different as a moonbeam from lightning, or frost from fire.'

She is impossibly caught between two conflicting forces within herself: the force that tells her she is made for Heathcliff and the force that wishes to be the greatest lady in the neighbourhood – which marriage to Edgar would make her. The intensity of her emotions is clear in this quotation (see p. 104 for the complete passage):

> Top ten quotation

'My love for Linton is like the foliage in the woods: time will change it, I'm well aware, as winter changes the trees. My love for Heathcliff resembles the eternal rocks beneath: a source of little visible delight, but necessary. Nelly, I am Heathcliff!'

Nelly Dean

Nelly Dean is a dedicated family servant. She has lived in and around the Earnshaw household since she was a girl herself, as her mother was Hindley's nurse-maid. She therefore knows the family intimately. As almost a member of the family, she is closely involved with all that occurs and she repeatedly inhabits the middle ground between warring factions. She bravely refuses to accept the status quo despite suffering for it both emotionally and physically. She is the primary narrator of the tale, and provides us with an overview of the complex unfolding events, offering a rationalising commentary. She has clearly been deeply affected and scarred by what has taken place at Thrushcross Grange and Wuthering Heights, having watched the steady disintegration and resurrection of the Earnshaw and Linton families over a long period of time.

Although she is a servant, Nelly is somehow different from the majority of household staff. Mr Lockwood makes this clear in Volume I, Chapter VII when he observes:

> 'Excepting a few provincialisms of slight consequence, you have no marks of the manners which I am habituated to consider as peculiar to your class. I am sure you have thought a great deal more than the generality of servants think.'

And Nelly demonstrates that she is an intelligent and thoughtful character when, with typical self-effacement she tells Mr Lockwood:

> 'I have undergone sharp discipline, which has taught me wisdom; and then, I have read more than you would fancy, Mr Lockwood. You could not open a book in this library that I have not looked into, and got something out of also …'

She is the repository of all the characters' secrets. Cathy and Heathcliff both confide in her and she bears their emotional baggage. She is repeatedly put in impossible positions, frequently finding herself imprisoned (sometimes literally) within her divided loyalties. Her commonsensical, no-nonsense viewpoint counterbalances the excesses and passions of the main characters and roots the novel in reality.

Nelly Dean is the repository of all the characters' secrets.

Build critical skills

Watch Juliette Binoche on YouTube as Cathy in the scene where she discusses her choice to marry Edgar with Nelly Dean (see p. 110 for the full weblink). How effectively do you feel this captures Cathy's dilemma at this point in the novel?

CRITICAL VIEWS

Critical views of Nelly Dean have varied. In the absence of mother figures, she takes on a semi-maternal role for many of the children (and adults) in the novel. Fraser (1965: 223–6) identifies how she is regularly confronted by various kinds of wickedness and must stand in opposition to these for the good of others. Charlotte Brontë, in her Preface to the novel asks us to see Nelly as 'a specimen of true benevolence and homely fidelity'. Van Ghent (1953) stresses Nelly's function as a centre of reliability in the shifting sands of the novel and comments on her objectivity. Similarly, Robert C. McKibben (1960: 168–9) holds the opinion that Nelly is 'the calm in the eye of the hurricane. Secure and unassailable in her limited universe …'. Other critics, however, such as Wayne Booth (1961), have pointed out that owing to her inextricable connection with the horrific events of the novel Nelly's narrative must be seen as unreliable, and James Hafley (1958: 199) has gone so far as to say that 'Ellen Dean is the villain of the piece, one of the consummate villains in English literature'.

TASK

Drawing on evidence from the novel, write a critical response to these points of view on Nelly Dean.

▲ Nelly Dean 'eating the knife' in Minnesota Opera's 2011 production of Bernard Herrmann's opera *Wuthering Heights*

Mr Lockwood

Mr Lockwood is an outsider in the rugged Yorkshire world. His position is clearly laid out for him by Nelly Dean:

Top ten quotation

'We don't in general take to foreigners here, Mr Lockwood, unless they take to us first.'

An interloper from the south, he is well-spoken, and at times comes across as rather vain and pompous. Mr Lockwood is not described for us physically, but tells us 'I knew, through experience, that I was tolerably attractive.' We know that he has been unsuccessful in love. This is, perhaps, the result of a rather introverted nature which may suggest he is cold and uncaring. He tells us that faced with the developing intimacy of his relations with a young woman at a seaside town he was unable to tell her of his feelings and 'shrunk icily into myself, like a snail' thus gaining for himself a 'reputation of deliberate heartlessness'. His name – Lockwood – might, indeed, be taken to indicate somebody closed, emotionally unavailable and resistant and as such not really fitted for intimate relationships. He is a man 'of the busy world', and finds life at the Grange rather restrictive. He is also refined and bookish: 'take my books away, and I should be desperate!' he says, and it is evident that he feels out of place in the harsh world of the Heights and the brutality of existence there.

As the frame narrator, Mr Lockwood holds an interesting position. He is part of Brontë's story (he meets several of the characters in person and encounters the ghost of Cathy in his nightmare) but at the same time he is somehow distanced from it. He has to rely on the knowledge of Nelly Dean in order to make sense of the world he has intruded upon. He is in many ways in the same position as us – an outsider who hears the tale through the synthesising voice of Nelly Dean. He shares our confusion, shock and outrage, distanced as he is from the happenings of Nelly's tale. He also serves as a foil to Heathcliff. A real gentleman – a man of manners and refinement – he contrasts with Heathcliff who, while a gentleman by social position, never attains the demeanour of a true gentleman. His sense of this difference is identified on the very first page of his journal when he writes 'Mr Heathcliff and I are such a suitable pair to divide the desolation between us.'

Taking it further

Read John T. Matthews' article 'Framing in *Wuthering Heights*' (*Texas Studies in Literature and Language*, Vol. 27, No. 1, Nineteenth-Century English Literature, pp. 25–61). Explain Matthews' ideas and then consider how you might apply them to a reading of the novel.

TASK

In 'Emily Brontë's Mr Lockwood' (*Nineteenth-Century Fiction*, Vol. 12, No. 4, pp. 315–20) George J. Worth writes:

> … *critics differ regarding the precise role which Lockwood plays in the novel. At one extreme, there is Mark Schorer, who sees the figure of Lockwood, the symbol of conventional emotion, as one of the chief means by which Emily Brontë's theme … is brought home to the reader. At the other, Mary Sinclair affirms that Lockwood is not, properly speaking, a character at all: he is purposely left a vague sketch by Emily Brontë, for 'he is a mere looker-on'.*

How do you respond to these differing critical views of Mr Lockwood?

Hindley

Hindley in many ways typifies the world of *Wuthering Heights*. He is reckless and tyrannical and places his own needs and desires before those of others. When Heathcliff arrives with Mr Earnshaw, Hindley reacts brutally to what he sees as a betrayal by his father and he takes every opportunity he can to vent his anger on Heathcliff. As the novel progresses, Hindley proves to be vengeful and bullying by nature and frequently resorts to drink. On one occasion he drops his son Hareton from the stairs and the boy is only saved by Heathcliff catching him. After his wife Frances' death, Hindley falls in with a bad crowd and his character becomes suddenly much darker. Cathy says 'Hindley is too reckless to select his acquaintance prudently.' He also becomes increasingly driven by greed: 'doubtless my brother's covetousness will prompt him to accept the terms [of Heathcliff's return to the Grange]', but he is also profligate – 'though what he grasps with one hand, he flings away with the other' (p. 100).

Linton

Linton is a weak and in many ways pathetic character. He shamelessly uses his physical condition to manipulate others. In spite of this, Brontë creates some sympathy for him. Linton is bullied mercilessly by his father. Heathcliff's only real interest in his son is as a means of winning Thrushcross Grange by forcing him into marriage with Catherine. Linton is helpless against Heathcliff, according to whom he is a 'whelp' and 'tin polished to ape a service of silver'. Nelly describes him as a 'selfish and disagreeable' young man and calls him 'an indulged plague of a child'.

Catherine

Catherine is in many ways very similar to Cathy. She is a beautiful young woman, 'high-spirited, but not rough'. She is sensitive and lively, with the 'capacity for intense attractions'. This latter characteristic proves to be both her undoing and her salvation. Her initial attraction to Linton, leaves her open to Heathcliff's greedy machinations. She is independent minded, like her mother, and wilfully disobeys her father's instruction to stay at home when he is away visiting Isabella, and in so doing she falls into Heathcliff's clutches. As a result of her treatment by Heathcliff, she changes radically and turns into the harridan we see at the Heights.

> Top ten quotation

> Catherine spoke with a kind of dreary triumph: she seemed to have made up her mind to enter into the spirit of her future family, and draw pleasure from the griefs of her enemies.

In her relationship with Hareton, however, her 'attractions' are better directed and she overcomes her initial abuse of him to see the deeper qualities he possesses, finding in him a suitable companion and a fruitful outlet for the loving side of her character.

Hareton

Hareton is a fearless and resilient young man. He experiences terrible treatment at the hands of Heathcliff who uses him as a means of taking out his revenge on Hindley. As a result, Hareton is left illiterate and unable to express himself. His anger and frustration often overflow into physical violence. Although Heathcliff maltreats Hareton, he recognises his fundamentally good and noble nature. He describes him as 'gold put to the use of paving stones', unlike Linton who is 'tin polished to ape a service of silver'. This prepares us for the changes that occur when he develops his relationship with Catherine. Nelly sums up these changes:

> His honest, warm, and intelligent nature shook off rapidly the clouds of ignorance and degradation in which it had been bred; and Catherine's sincere commendations acted as a spur to his industry. His brightening mind brightened his features, and added spirit and nobility to their aspect – I could hardly fancy it the same individual …

Isabella

Isabella is perhaps the weakest of Brontë's female characters in *Wuthering Heights,* and she arguably suffers the most at the hands of Heathcliff. She proves naïve and headstrong, wilfully marrying Heathcliff against the advice of Nelly, Cathy and Edgar and pays heavily for it as she suffers dreadful brutality from Heathcliff. She has a romantic (and Romantic) view of life, which leads her into self-deluding fantasies. Heathcliff picks up on this. He knows that she pictures him as 'a hero of romance' and he cannot believe her naivety:

> 'I can hardly regard her in the light of a rational creature, so obstinately has she persisted in forming a fabulous notion of my character and acting on the false impressions she cherished. But, at last, I think she begins to know me'

Her choices leave her a shattered woman and eventually she flees the Heights, another victim in the feud between Heathcliff and Edgar. She pays the price of her independence, abandoned by both men and left profoundly isolated.

CRITICAL VIEW

The very words 'Gothic heroine' immediately conjure up a wealth of images for the modern reader: a young, attractive woman (virginity required) running in terror through an old, dark, crumbling mansion in the middle of nowhere, from either a psychotic man or a supernatural demon. She is always terminally helpless and more than a bit screechy, but is inevitably 'saved' by the good guy/future husband in the nick of time.

(Ellen Moers, *The Female Gothic*, 1977)

Build critical skills

Joseph and Zillah are the only two characters in the novel with biblical names – with the exception of the preacher Jabez Branderham who features in Mr Lockwood's dream in Volume I, Chapter III. Why do you think this is?

Joseph

Joseph is a cruel, cold-hearted, religious hypocrite, and Heathcliff's faithful servant. He is described by Mr Lockwood as 'hale and sinewy' and later as 'vinegar-faced': these adjectives capture the hard and twisted nature of the man.

Zillah

Zillah is another loyal servant at the Heights; quieter and apparently less cruel than Joseph, she nevertheless does nothing to try to help the victims of Heathcliff's barbarity. Nelly describes her as 'a narrow-minded, selfish woman', though this is perhaps understandable given that her master is Heathcliff.

Frances

Frances' background is rather unclear and Nelly Dean evidently feels ambiguous towards her. 'What she was, and where she was from he [Hindley] never informed us', she says. Hindley meets and marries her when he is away from the Heights at college. She appears to be rather an immature and flighty individual: 'Every object she saw, the moment she crossed the threshold, appeared to delight her; … I thought she was half silly'. She is attractive and lively, 'young, and fresh-complexioned, and her eyes sparkled as bright as diamonds', but Nelly feels 'no impulse to sympathise with her.'

Mr Earnshaw

Mr Earnshaw is a strict and humourless man. When he brings Heathcliff back from a business trip to Liverpool he sets in motion a train of events that will change the world of the Grange and the Heights forever. He exacerbates this situation by favouring Heathcliff over his own son, Hindley.

Build critical skills

In his review of Alex Woloch's book *The One vs. the Many: Minor Characters and the Space of the Protagonist in the Novel*, David Brewer writes:

> *Each and every figure in a novel is (at least theoretically) as rich and complex and potentially compelling an individual as the protagonist. When minor characters are given less time on-page than they deserve, the result is distortion and caricature, a flattening that makes the protagonist's roundness possible.*

How do you respond to this idea in relation to the minor (and major) characters in *Wuthering Heights*?

Mrs Earnshaw

As Cathy and Hindley's mother, Mrs Earnshaw is unhappy about her husband bringing Heathcliff into the household at the Heights.

Mr Linton

A magistrate and the owner of Thrushcross Grange, Mr Linton is the social superior of the Earnshaws. He is basically a kind man, however, and looks after Cathy when she falls ill at his house.

Mrs Linton

A kindly woman, Mrs Linton dislikes Heathcliff and wishes to help Cathy develop into a proper young lady. She catches Cathy's fever when Cathy is staying at the Grange and dies from it.

Mr Green

Mr Green is Edgar's lawyer, but proves disloyal. When Edgar summons Mr Green to amend his will to prevent Heathcliff from inheriting Thrushcross Grange, Green at Heathcliff's instigation, deliberately delays his journey and Edgar dies before he can make the change.

Mr Kenneth

The doctor from Gimmerton, Mr Kenneth is a frank, 'plain, rough man' and is one of Hindley's drinking companions. He attends a number of the key events of the novel: Hareton's birth, Cathy's illness, Hindley's death, Edgar's death, and Heathcliff's final illness. He also treats Mr Lockwood and tells Nelly of a late-night meeting between Heathcliff and Isabella in Volume I, Chapter XII.

Taking it further ▶▶

Read C.P. Sanger's essay 'The Structure of *Wuthering Heights*' (1926) in which he explores Emily Brontë's use of the law in the novel.

Writer's methods: form, structure and language

Target your thinking

- How does Brontë develop her themes, settings and characters as the novel unfolds? (**AO1**)
- What dramatic methods does Brontë use to shape the reader's responses at crucial points in the narrative? (**AO2**)

Narrative perspective

When we think about the form of *Wuthering Heights* we are referring to the choices that Emily Brontë makes about how to tell her story. The key issue here is viewpoint – sometimes known as narrative perspective. For example, Brontë could have written the story in the third person. In that case, the narrator would not have been one of the central characters in the tale. This would have allowed her to achieve certain effects. Third person narrators, for instance, often have a privileged position – they usually know things that the reader and the characters in the story do not know themselves. Sometimes these third person narrators have almost god-like knowledge (these are known as omniscient narrators); they know, for example, how characters are feeling and why they do the things they do. On other occasions the third person voice is given to a narrator with more limited insight (a limited third person narrator), but even where this is the case, they still have a distance from the events of the tale that allows them to provide readers with an overview.

Instead of opting for a third person narrator, Brontë chooses to use a variety of first person narrators of greater or lesser importance. First person narrators are always in some way a participant in the tale they tell, even if this is only in a limited way (as is the case with Mr Lockwood). First person narrators provide readers with very personal and immediate narratives and they offer their own personal perspectives on the events they relate. Brontë uses multiple first person narratives in *Wuthering Heights*.

The use of a first person narrator comes with certain benefits: it can create closeness, affection and empathy. As readers view events from one character's perspective, the author can control the ways in which readers see and understand what is happening. Through first person narratives, readers can be given detailed insight into characters' situations and motivations. On the other hand, seeing events from one character's point of view also comes with certain risks. Readers might be given a biased or unreliable account of events. Reading first person narratives therefore needs to come with a health warning: you cannot necessarily trust either the person telling the story or the story they tell.

Taking it further ▶

Tzvetan Todorov makes a distinction in narratives between the content of a story (*fabula*) and the way it is ordered, organised and presented — its plot (*sjuzet*). He goes on to explain that this requires readers to think about a number of things:

- ▶ Who is the teller of the tale?
- ▶ What relationship does the teller have with their immediate audience (characters to whom they are speaking or writing within the tale they are telling) and with the distant audience (the reader)? What relationship, for example, does Nelly Dean have with the inhabitants of the Heights and the Grange? What relationship does she have with the reader? How about Mr Lockwood? Who is the imagined 'reader' of his journal?
- ▶ How is the story told?
- ▶ What is explicitly told, what is implied and what is omitted?
- ▶ What values does the story convey?
- ▶ How does the teller feel about the story they are telling?

How do you relate this idea to the various narratives of *Wuthering Heights*?

Reliability

It is always important to consider how far we, as readers, can rely on the person telling us the tale. In order to do this it is important to evaluate:

- ◥ what the narrator is telling
- ◥ how they are telling it
- ◥ why they are telling it
- ◥ to whom they are telling it.

A narrator readers cannot trust is known as an **unreliable narrator**. They may be unreliable for a variety of reasons:

- ◥ They do not know all the facts.
- ◥ They have a limited understanding of events (for example, they are a child).
- ◥ It is not safe for them to give an honest account.
- ◥ They are trying to deceive themselves.
- ◥ They are deliberately trying to deceive their audience.

Narrative structure

The narrative structure of *Wuthering Heights* is complex. The tale is narrated from multiple perspectives and all of the narrators are in one way or another involved in the tale they tell. The diagram below demonstrates how the different narratives relate to each other.

> **Build critical skills**
>
> To what extent do you think the narrators in *Wuthering Heights* – both major and minor – are reliable? Why do you think this?

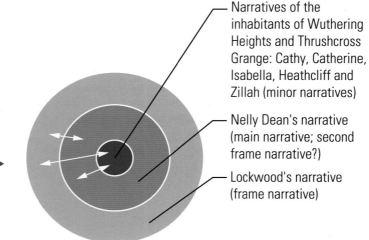

Narratives of the inhabitants of Wuthering Heights and Thrushcross Grange: Cathy, Catherine, Isabella, Heathcliff and Zillah (minor narratives)

Nelly Dean's narrative (main narrative; second frame narrative?)

Lockwood's narrative (frame narrative)

The narrative structure ▶ of *Wuthering Heights*: the arrows on the diagram indicate the links that exist between the various narratives

At the outer edge of the diagram we have Mr Lockwood's frame narrative. When he arrives at Thrushcross Grange in 1801 he becomes a part of the final stages of the tale of the Lintons and the Earnshaws. As Heathcliff's tenant he is to a limited extent involved in events, but acts largely as an outsider whose tale 'frames' the main narrative which, it transpires, actually commences in 1771.

Nelly Dean is the main narrator, knowing as she does the whole story. As a long-term resident, she knows both the Heights and the Grange and the families in each household very well. She is in many ways a significant participant in the events she tells, but it is important to note that her narrative, like Mr Lockwood's, also serves something of a framing function; her own narrative incorporates sub-narrative elements from Cathy, Catherine, Isabella, Heathcliff and Zillah. The narratives of these characters, sometimes oral narratives and sometimes in the form of letters, are important in developing the readers' perspective on events at the Heights and the Grange, but these characters may be considered as minor narrators.

Taking it further ▶

Read 'Gender and Layered Narrative in *Wuthering Heights* and *The Tenant of Wildfell Hall*' by N.M. Jacobs (in *The Brontës*, ed. Patricia Ingham, 2003). To what extent do you find Jacobs' views helpful?

TASK

Herman, Jahn and Ryan (2005: 369) refer to *Wuthering Heights* as a classic example of the **multiple embedded narrative**. They identify important questions about the relationship between the various narrative layers of the novel and how these colour the reader's view of what is happening:

The reader may well wonder whether it is more important that we are reading what Isabella said, or what Nelly says she said, or what Mr Lockwood says Nelly said she said.

Write your reponse to this idea in relation to the novel and its narrative structure.

Narrative voices

A number of different aspects make the 'voice' of a narrator unique:

- **Vocabulary**: the words a narrator uses. These often provide an interesting insight into the narrator (such as their education, their gender, their social class, their interests, the ways in which they see and try to represent the world). Does their vocabulary vary according to whom they are addressing?

- **Style**: the level of formality of a narrator's language. Again this can help to understand the narrator (the ways in which they want to present themselves, their position, the reason why they are telling the story, the ways in which they want their story to appear, their perception of their audience and their relationship with that audience).

- **Syntax**: the ways in which narrators construct their sentences. Thinking about the variety and frequency of sentence types used by narrators provides insight (Do they use largely simple sentences or do they use more complex and compound sentences? Do they use sentence types to create different effects at different points in their narrative? Does their sentence structure vary according to whom they are addressing? What might this tell us about the narrator?)

- **Form**: the means narrators use to express themselves. Narrators may adopt a variety of different forms (such as journals, letters, dialogue, confession). The form a narrator adopts to tell a tale affects the tale itself. What might it also tell us about the narrator?

> **TASK**
>
> What differences do you notice about the narrative voices of Mr Lockwood and Nelly Dean? What about the minor narrators – Cathy, Catherine, Isabella, Heathcliff and Zillah? Which parts of the tale do they tell? Use vocabulary, style, syntax and form as a way of analysing narrative voice.

Motifs

A motif is a recurring image or idea in a literary work. Less pervasive than what we might consider a theme, a motif is nevertheless a significant means by which writers seek to convey meaning to their readers.

Landscape and buildings

The rugged Yorkshire setting, with its violent weather and harsh landscape, reflects the events of the novel. The isolated location represents the isolation of the characters, and provides a suitable wild and violent backdrop – it is a place beyond the bounds of conventional society and its demands. Mr Lockwood's initial description of the Heights is immediately striking. The grotesque detail of the carvings of 'a wilderness of crumbling griffins, and shameless little boys' speaks of bizarre excess, and the inscription dating the house to 1500 gives the building a feeling of brooding permanence. The tantalising name of Earnshaw presides over the entrance to the dark halls of the house and the family history it embodies. This detail is confusing for us, as we have just learnt that the house is owned by Heathcliff. Physically, the house is set in a landscape of punishing, volatile weather, the symbolic significance of which soon becomes apparent.

The house is unlike other houses in the area, set apart by its physical location and its nature. We are impressed by its grandeur (e.g. words like 'lavished'), but cannot escape the forbidding and mysterious overtones of the word 'penetralium', which encapsulates a world of dark threat. The nameless voice coming from 'deep within' adds to Mr Lockwood's feelings of threat and the overpowering towers of tankards and lack of cooking utensils suggest a world where drinking is rife and where home comforts are lacking. The deep, narrow windows are like squinting, deep-set eyes, threateningly watching the inhabitants. Lurking dogs create a forbidding air, heavy colours ('gaudy', 'green', 'black') add to the sense of gloom, and violence is suggested by the weapons. The dreadful nature of the Heights is also emphasised by Isabella:

> 'far rather would I be condemned to a perpetual dwelling in the infernal regions, than even for one night abide beneath the roof of Wuthering Heights again.'

Top ten quotation

Taking it further ▶

Think of other texts you have studied for A-level or that you have read for pleasure where location is significant. In what ways are the effects they achieve similar to *Wuthering Heights* and in what ways are they different?

The depiction of Heathcliff's room provides another excellent example of Brontë's use of location. It captures something of his mysterious complexity. The carpet is 'a good one', indicating that Heathcliff has good qualities, yet the panels of the wall are 'deformed' as, perhaps, Heathcliff's nature has been deformed by maltreatment. The decayed wealth of the chamber might be taken to symbolise the degradation of Heathcliff and his house, where the potential for nobility and grandeur have fallen into shabby disrepair. The dust that is everywhere in the room suggests death and decay, while the emphasis on the colour crimson and the tattered red curtains could represent blood and violence. The room has been violently ill-used, reflecting the maltreatment Heathcliff suffered as a child and the destruction he has wreaked on those around him.

> ### TASK
> Take another significant room or location in the novel and write your own detailed description of it, trying to use features typical of Brontë's form, structure and language. Afterwards, think carefully about what you have learnt about Brontë's style.

Elsewhere, Brontë uses the landscape as a way of reflecting and representing character:

> Catherine's face was just like the landscape – shadows and sunshine flitting over it, in rapid succession; but the shadows rested longer and the sunshine was more transient, and her poor little heart reproached itself for even that passing forgetfulness of its cares.

Top ten quotation

The link between landscape and Catherine's psychological state is explicit. The rugged beauty and the harshness of the place are both represented in her psyche. And we recall that earlier in the novel Cathy sought to define both Edgar and Heathcliff in terms of the landscape and the natural world.

At the very end of the novel, as at its very beginning, Mr Lockwood reflects on the Yorkshire landscape. Instead of the prohibitive Wuthering Heights and stormy weather, however, here his focus is on the churchyard and the fine conditions. The churchyard is a symbolic location. The natural world and the graves are used as a means of capturing the three central characters of the novel and their complex relationships – the socially acceptable Edgar lies 'in' the sanctified, tended land of the graveyard; Cathy, more suspect, lies half 'in' and half 'out'; the social and moral outcast, Heathcliff, lies totally 'out'.

CRITICAL VIEW

In *An Introduction to the English Novel* (1951) the Marxist critic Arnold Kettle is at pains to emphasise the material reality of the novel:

> Wuthering Heights *is about England in 1847. The people it reveals are not in a never-never land, but in Yorkshire. Heathcliff was not born in the pages of Byron, but in a Liverpool slum. The language of Nelly, Joseph and Hareton is the language of the Yorkshire people. The story of* Wuthering Heights *is concerned not with love in the abstract but with the passions of living people, with property ownership, the attraction of social comforts, the arrangement of marriages, the importance of education, the validity of religion, the relations of rich and poor.*

How do you respond to this as a view of the novel?

Journeys

Physical journeys are inextricably linked to the spiritual and psychological journeys that characters are engaged upon. Mr Earnshaw travels to Liverpool, bringing Heathcliff back with him, and setting in train the psychological journeys of the residents of the Heights and the Grange. Mr Lockwood and Heathcliff arrive in Yorkshire only to begin further journeys of self-discovery. Isabella travels to the south to escape the journey of her violent marriage with Heathcliff, and Linton undertakes an enforced trip of personal discovery when he returns to Yorkshire after Isabella dies.

Apart from a few exceptional long journeys, movement within the text occurs within the limited locale of the Grange and the Heights. Brontë does not specify a distance, but it is clear that Gimmerton, the nearest village, is some distance away. This emphasises the loneliness of existence on the moors. The majority of the traffic in the novel is between the Heights and the Grange. Brontë uses the loneliness and lack of movement to intensify the atmosphere.

CRITICAL VIEW

It manages to be a number of things: a romance that brilliantly challenges the basic presumptions of the 'romantic'; a 'gothic' that evolves – with an absolutely inevitable grace – into its temperamental opposite; a parable of innocence and loss, and childhood's necessary defeat …

(Joyce Carol Oates, 1983)

Here Oates suggests three other types of 'journey' in genre terms. How do you relate to these as perspectives on the novel?

Given the significance of location and journey in the text, it is important to consider the structural 'journey' that Brontë employs, too. *Wuthering Heights* traces a set of intertwined journeys. Mr Lockwood's journey to the north and his resulting contact with the almost other-worldly events at the Heights and the Grange take him to the dark heart of human nature, a place that he then leaves, but to which he significantly returns at the end of the tale, providing a satisfying, cyclical conclusion. The structural interdependency of the various narratives, filtered through the centralising consciousness of Nelly Dean, provides a forceful logic to the tale. Nelly's unique perspective allows her to map the 'journey' of the two houses, as the Earnshaws and the Lintons are gradually drawn together by the forces of intermarriage and time.

The journey ends fittingly with a vision of three graves. The reader and Mr Lockwood face the tombs of Edgar, Cathy and Heathcliff on the boundary of the churchyard and the moor. The setting of this final scene is highly suggestive – we are on the borders of the tame and the wild, the holy and the unholy, the dead and the living, the lover and the beloved, the elevated and the earthly, the spiritual and the bodily. It has been a journey from life to death, but also from death to life; from love to hate, but also from hate to love. Brontë's narrative has been a journey of ambiguity, which is reflected in this final choice of location.

Blood

Blood develops a set of powerful overtones as the novel progresses. Blood is also linked to sex and sexual excess in *Wuthering Heights*. A particularly striking example comes when Heathcliff nearly kills Hareton after he returns from visiting Cathy's grave and forces Joseph to kneel in the midst of the pool of blood. The letting of blood here symbolises Heathcliff's pent-up sexual frustration. The novel abounds in examples of bloodshed, and it takes on an almost ritual significance. In addition, the repeated emphasis on blood is connected in the reader's mind to the concept of revenge.

Ideas of blood-relationship and bloodline are also significant in the novel. *Wuthering Heights* traces the coming together of two houses. The mingling of Earnshaw and Linton blood is highly significant, especially in terms of Heathcliff's claims upon Thrushcross Grange. It is with the marriage of Catherine

Context

In many Gothic texts (such as *Dracula* and *Frankenstein*), blood and sexual fluids become closely related, and in the case of *Dracula* they become almost interchangeable. This is captured neatly in *The Handbook to Gothic Literature* (Mulvey-Roberts, 1998) which refers to 'the subtle cultural equation of blood and semen - the figurative and literal carriers of racial and individual qualities'.

and Hareton that union is finally achieved – both of blood and of purpose. The idea of blood connection and family is particularly potent in Gothic fiction. As Laura Kranzler observes, the idea of family, sex and generation is a powerful motif, breeding the fear of 'generational repetition'.

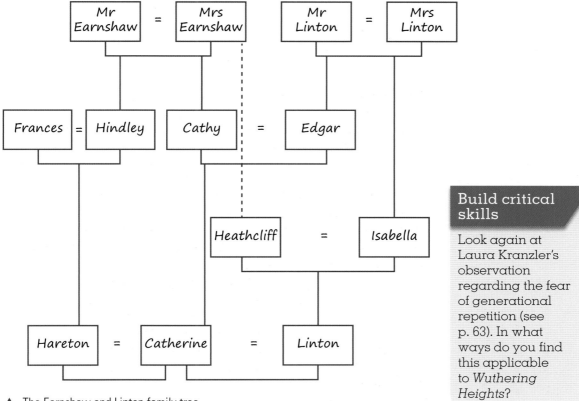

▲ The Earnshaw and Linton family tree

Build critical skills

Look again at Laura Kranzler's observation regarding the fear of generational repetition (see p. 63). In what ways do you find this applicable to *Wuthering Heights*?

Doubling of characters

This device has a significant impact on the structure and effect of the novel. Names are repeated across the generations, creating a confusing and complex set of interrelations. The uncertainties this generates mirror the doubt, insecurity and repetition faced by the characters themselves. It also links to a significant component of Gothic fiction – the fear and apparent inevitability of generational repetition. Repeatedly we see how violence and characteristics descend from one generation to another of the Earnshaws and the Lintons. Doublings are not fixed, and frequently shift as the novel progresses, creating a range of effects and emphasising both similarities and differences between the characters that are paired.

Cathy and Heathcliff

These two characters are allied so closely as to appear virtually complementary halves of the same character. Brontë emphasises the extreme closeness between Cathy and Heathcliff, most famously in Cathy's assertion that 'I am Heathcliff!'. They are incapable of living without one another, but also unable to coexist happily. They are, in many ways, destructively alike. Their relationship reflects this contradictory state of affairs – love/hate, desire to possess/desire to break free, healing/wounding. While brutally physical on occasions, the alliance is never consummated; rather it is deeply spiritual. On the whole, it is an unfulfilled relationship – even when reunited in death, their connection is somehow 'unholy' and incomplete, in that their spirits cannot rest.

Their relationship is elemental and absolute; enduring, hard and unchangeable. Their union is spiritual rather than physical. Brontë's language conveys the power of Cathy's and Heathcliff's feelings. Their natures and self-worth are entirely bound up with each other, and they define their existence by each other. This pairing is not a source of happiness (see Kristeva's views on p. 35). There is 'little visible delight' in their relationship, and more frequently there is great torment. Cathy's description of Heathcliff as 'my all in all' (p. 125) further emphasises their mutual dependence. The loss of her 'all' when she marries Edgar has a profound effect. Similarly, when Cathy dies both are condemned to unrest and heart-rending sorrow as if they have lost the greater part of themselves in losing each other.

Cathy and Heathcliff are tied together by such powerful spiritual bonds that they haunt one another. Until they are reunited in death, no personal completion is possible. Note how Cathy drives Heathcliff on, insisting that he call up the spirits in the churchyard. In the same way, it is her continual hauntings that pull Heathcliff into final union with her. Her determination and force of character are clear in her language – she envisages herself buried at double the conventional depth and covered by the weight of the entire church. Such language is fully in keeping with the extreme nature of her character and the power of her feelings for Heathcliff.

When Cathy and Heathcliff are reunited after Heathcliff's return to Yorkshire, so extreme is their reaction that Nelly Dean doubts Cathy is a 'creature of my own species' (p. 162). We are struck by the feral intensity of this reunion. It is more like a battle between wild beasts than a meeting of lovers. Brontë's vocabulary embodies excess and uncontrollable emotion: Nelly fears that the shock of such a meeting may kill Cathy. Their passion is wordless, expressed in violent physicality, and takes them to the borders of sanity and humanity.

Although in many respects so close, Cathy and Heathcliff are also significantly different and do much to hurt each other. The need to wound each other springs from the impossibility of their pairing. The infliction of psychological and physical pain represents a pathological need to punish and to be punished.

Neither is suited to marriage and domesticity, and such a coupling would not be sustainable. Cathy, talking to Nelly Dean, recognises that union with Heathcliff and marriage to him are two entirely distinct issues. She admits the passion and extreme personal closeness between them, but cannot and will not marry him:

> 'It would degrade me to marry Heathcliff, now; so he shall never know how I love him; and that, not because he's handsome, Nelly, but because he's more myself than I am. Whatever our souls are made of, his and mine are the same, and Linton's is as different as a moonbeam from lightning, or frost from fire.' (p. 81)

At the same time as she denies earthly union (marriage), however, she perversely yearns for eternal union:

> 'I wish I could hold you,' she continued, bitterly, 'till we were both dead! I shouldn't care what you suffered. I care nothing for your sufferings. Why shouldn't you suffer? I do!' (p. 160)

These contradictory impulses illustrate the complexity of their pairing.

TASK

Explain how each of these significant moments in Cathy and Heathcliff's relationship develops our perspective:

- Cathy's visitation on the night Mr Lockwood stays at the Heights
- Cathy's 'capture' by the Lintons and her stay at the Grange
- Cathy's explanation to Nelly of why she cannot marry Heathcliff
- Cathy's marriage to Edgar
- Cathy's illness and madness
- Cathy's death
- Heathcliff's recognition of the similarity of both Hareton and Catherine to his Cathy
- Heathcliff's death.

Mr Lockwood and Heathcliff

Mr Lockwood immediately establishes the pairing of himself and Heathcliff: 'Mr Heathcliff and I are such a suitable pair to divide the desolation between us.' (p. 3). We may assume initially that this indicates a similarity between the two men. However, it quickly becomes apparent that there is a profound difference between Mr Lockwood and his landlord. Mr Lockwood represents social acceptability and gentility. Heathcliff, on the other hand, is technically a gentleman, but actually an upstart, distinctly lacking in gentility. They form the last in a long line of oppositions between the householders of the Heights and the Grange.

Cathy and Catherine

Cathy and Catherine are both independent in spirit and capable of great personal strength, as well as being perpetrators of psychological cruelty. Their lives and marriages parallel one another significantly. Catherine appears to be a more controlled version of her mother. She is, after all, a combination of Earnshaw and Linton blood. Catherine's life in a sense offers a second chance at happiness after the sad dissatisfaction of Cathy's. This is suggested structurally within the novel itself, as the second half of the book (subsequent to the death of Cathy) substantially reflects the first half.

Heathcliff and Hindley

Heathcliff and Hindley are in many ways reflections of each other. Hindley systematically mistreats Heathcliff after the death of Mr Earnshaw, because he resents his father's introduction of the socially suspect outsider Heathcliff into the household. As an act of revenge, Heathcliff determines to brutalise Hareton, Hindley's son.

Heathcliff and Hareton

Heathcliff is made into a brute by the treatment of Hindley, and so, in his turn, Hareton is brutalised by Heathcliff. There is a grudging respect between them in their similarity.

Heathcliff and Linton

Both Heathcliff and Linton come to the Heights as outsiders; Heathcliff from Liverpool and Linton from the south by Edgar after Isabella's death. Both have a natural ability to manipulate. They are clearly opposites too: Heathcliff is a powerful and domineering man, while Linton is sickly and easily dominated. Linton lacks his father's saving graces – Heathcliff does not appear naturally unpleasant, but is made so.

Heathcliff and Edgar

Heathcliff and Edgar are rivals for Cathy's hand. They are distinct opposites: Heathcliff is wild, a risk-taker and passionate in both love and hate; Edgar is cultivated, always errs on the side of safety, and is usually restrained in his emotional reactions. They are strangely united, however, in their life-long rivalry over Cathy. The focus of this enmity transfers, after Cathy's death, onto the desire to possess the Grange and Catherine.

Linton and Hareton

Linton and Hareton are opposites. Linton is a weak, manipulative, and selfish youth; Hareton, on the other hand, is resilient, frank, naturally kind and often thinks of others. Both appear, in a sense, as 'sons' of Heathcliff as both marry Catherine. Her forced marriage to Linton, which is a tool in Heathcliff's plot to gain control of the Grange, and her marriage of love to Hareton can be related to the changes that occur in the novel as the older generation dies out and a new era of more peaceful relations between the Linton and Earnshaw families emerges.

Catherine Linton/Catherine Earnshaw/ Catherine Heathcliff

Brontë deliberately sets up a confusion over identity early in the novel when Mr Lockwood finds scratched into the wood of his disturbingly claustrophobic bed the names Catherine Linton, Catherine Earnshaw and Catherine Heathcliff. Unsurprisingly, he is bewildered. Like him, we are plunged into the unfamiliar and distressing world of the Heights and the uncertainty created by these three names deepens this. The names represent the concept of generational repetition that is to be so important to the text. They also alert the reader to the important idea of the divided personality (see the Freudian reading of the novel on p. 81 of this guide) and to the often uncertain distinction between characters in Brontë's fictional world. Such uncertainties are multiplied when we consider that both Cathy and Catherine may be said to hold each of these three names in the course of the tale. Cathy is born an Earnshaw, marries Edgar Linton and, although she never in fact takes his name, says, 'I am Heathcliff'. Catherine is born a Linton, marries Linton Heathcliff and then marries Hareton Earnshaw.

Doubling of events

The pairing of characters and doubling of events are related devices. Similarities and contrasts between characters are frequently revealed by their exposure to the same or similar circumstances. Repetition and paralleling of events emphasises the cycle of brutality and self-destruction that characterises the Linton and Earnshaw families. Repetition can also lead to improvement. This encourages us to hope for change. Reflecting this structurally, the novel falls into two halves – the story of Cathy, Edgar and Heathcliff is told in the first half, and the balancing tale of Catherine, Hareton and Linton in the second. While we remain aware of the similarities between Cathy and Catherine and the strange triangular relationships in which both find themselves, we always remain alert to the possibility that Catherine's story may represent a second chance – the victory of hope, fulfilment and happiness over sadness and disappointment.

> **Build critical skills**
>
> Where, in your view, does the division between the first and second half of the novel come? Is it really at the end of Volume I?

TASK

Brontë mirrors events and motifs in both halves of the novel (locks of hair, window scenes, outsiders, etc.). Make a list of these and make notes on how each contributes to the effect of the novel.

CRITICAL VIEW

The idea that Gothic provides a dark mirror to reality is propounded by Laura Kranzler (2000):

> [The] juxtaposition of the ghastly and the everyday suggests one of the defining characteristics of the gothic genre, that of the uncanny double, the shadowy world that is the complex underbelly of familiar experience.

Brontë holds both of these potential outcomes in the balance, and we remain uncertain of which will triumph until the very end. Uncertainty is created as Heathcliff, Edgar (and arguably Cathy, from beyond the grave) remain alive throughout both halves of the tale and are active players in both. The fates of both the older generation and the younger generation are locked together.

Language

Opposites and extremes

As we have seen, *Wuthering Heights* is closely related to the Gothic genre. Opposition and contraries play a central part in exploring liminal states, and many of the situations the characters face in the course of the novel make use of such opposites. Brontë's language naturally reflects this. Gothic dualisms are more fully outlined on page 73 of this guide. Often, in order to explore the contradictory and violently shifting nature of her tale, her language veers from one extreme to another.

Good and evil

The ultimate contrast, in terms of the Christian tradition within which the novel operates, is the contrast between heaven, the perfection of union with God, and hell, the eternal torment of separation from God. Brontë's language reflects the division between heaven and hell. Note particularly her use of the language of hell and things hellish in reference to Heathcliff, who is repeatedly referred to as 'the fiend' and as 'diabolical'.

The Bible

Brontë's language frequently reflects the biblical concepts dealt with in *Wuthering Heights*. Key biblical concepts such as high places, sheep and wolves are all reflected in the language of the novel, and make a significant impact. They import an authoritative tone into the fabric of the novel, adding to our sense of foreboding.

Romance

The triangular romances between Heathcliff and Cathy and Edgar, and Linton and Catherine and Hareton are an important part of the novel. Brontë's language in this respect is, as we would expect, far from conventional, as the romances she presents are far from conventional. It is useful to examine the words she uses to describe the 'good' romances between Cathy and Edgar and Catherine and Hareton and to compare these to the language associated with the 'bad' romances between Cathy and Heathcliff and Catherine and Linton.

Dialect and Standard English

Although it is not a dialect novel, *Wuthering Heights* does make use of the colourful Yorkshire dialect. Characters such as Zillah and Joseph speak in dialect, which is used as a clear marker of social distinctions. The more socially elevated characters such as Mr Lockwood, Edgar and others do not employ any dialect, but speak using Standard English. Indeed, Mr Lockwood specifically identifies dialect variation as an issue for us when he tells us the local meaning of the word 'wuthering'. It is important to look closely at where Brontë employs dialect and the social distinctions she creates by using it.

Symbolism

Brontë employs certain key symbols throughout *Wuthering Heights*:

- windows
- walls
- eyes
- storms
- the graveyard
- the moors.

Animal vocabulary

Brontë employs animal imagery and related vocabulary throughout the novel. This reflects the brutally violent world of the tale. Heathcliff and Cathy are both frequently compared to animals, and this suggests their feral, uncontrolled natures. Near the beginning of the novel, dogs are used to create the brooding threat of the Heights and to represent the fear Mr Lockwood experiences on his visit there. The repeated images of sheep and wolves also relate specifically to the biblical use of animals.

> **Build critical skills**
>
> Choose one or more of the symbols Brontë uses. List examples and explain what they represent and how the symbol is used in the course of the novel.

Contexts

Target your thinking

- What different critical positions might be applied to *Wuthering Heights* to extend your knowledge of the text? (**AO1**)
- How can setting *Wuthering Heights* within a broad range of contexts deepen your understanding of the novel and the ways in which different readers might respond to it? (**AO3**)
- What links might be traced between *Wuthering Heights* and various other literary texts and literary movements? (**AO4**)
- What links might be traced between *Wuthering Heights* and various social and historical contexts? (**AO4**)
- How can applying various critical approaches enrich your understanding of *Wuthering Heights* and the ways in which different readers might interpret it? (**AO5**)

Biographical context

Emily Brontë timeline

1818	30 July, born at Thornton, near Bradford, Yorkshire.
1820	April, the Brontë family moves to Haworth.
1821	September, mother dies.
1824	November, attends Cowan Bridge School.
1825	Two older sisters die; Charlotte and Emily leave Cowan Bridge.
1831	Emily and Anne begin their imaginary Gondal saga.
1834	Earliest dated Emily Brontë manuscript.
1836	Earliest dated poem.
1837	Teaches at Law Hill School; remains there about six months.

1838–42	Over half of Emily's surviving poems written.
1842	Spends ten months at school in Brussels with Charlotte; returns to Haworth after the death of Aunt Branwell.
1845	Charlotte and Emily collaborate on a volume of poems; begins *Wuthering Heights*.
1846	Poems by Currer, Ellis and Acton Bell published; *Wuthering Heights* completed.
1847	*Wuthering Heights* published.
1848	September, Branwell dies; Emily leaves home for the last time to attend his funeral; 19 December, Emily dies.
1850	*Wuthering Heights* reissued, with a selection of poems and a biographical notice by Charlotte.
1941	Hatfield's edition of *The Complete Poems of Emily Jane Brontë* published.

▲ A timeline of Emily Brontë's life

Biographical sketch

Emily Brontë was the fifth of six children born to the Reverend Patrick Brontë, a stern evangelical curate, and his wife Maria. Emily was only three years old when her mother died of cancer, after which Emily and her five siblings were brought up by their father and their Aunt Branwell, a strict Calvinist, who moved in to help the family. They lived in a parsonage in Haworth with the bleak moors of Yorkshire on one side and the parish graveyard on the other.

◀ The Brontës' parsonage, viewed from the graveyard

From the age of six, Emily attended a boarding school, where her sisters were already enrolled. The school was run with the intention of punishing the pupils' bodies in order that their souls might be saved. The students were hungry, cold, tired, and often ill. After the deaths of their older sisters from tuberculosis, Charlotte and Emily returned to Haworth, where they spent the rest of their childhood with their father, their sister Anne and their notoriously wild and mysterious brother, Branwell, isolated on the beautiful but inhospitable moors.

Emily rarely spent any time away from home. In 1835, at the age of 17, she went to Roe Head School, where Charlotte was teaching, but became so ill that her sister was convinced she would die unless she returned home. She left home in 1837 and in 1842, on the latter occasion to study in Belgium, but both times was unable to bear a long separation from her beloved, wild homeland. She could not adapt to the demands of living the life of a genteel Victorian lady, nor could she ever fit in fully with strangers. She never made any close friends outside her family circle.

Applying biography

Applying biographical or autobiographical information to a writer's work can be both an interesting and an illuminating exercise, although we should always be careful when doing so. The following list indicates how the events of Brontë's life find their way into the fictional world of *Wuthering Heights*:

- ◥ Isolated locations, so much a part of Brontë's home life, are a central feature in the novel.

- ◥ Brontë's harsh school experience is echoed everywhere in the novel; brutality forms a key part of the 'education' of both Heathcliff and Hareton, who are taught their place and deliberately kept in ignorance. There is also a significant difference to draw here between the apparently more educated and refined Lintons and the 'civilised' life at the Grange, and the more brutal and unrefined Heights. Later in the novel, Catherine's caring 'education' of Hareton is essential in restoring peace.

- ◥ Brontë's strict religious background is mirrored in the religious hypocrisy of Joseph and in Mr Lockwood's dream of the fanatical preacher, Jabez Branderham. Given the strictness of her upbringing, we might be surprised at the dark, irreligious nature of Brontë's tale, or indeed we may see in that upbringing the reason for it.

- ◥ Brontë never enjoyed the experience of travelling from home. The outside world (even nearby Gimmerton) and its representatives are viewed with suspicion. Journeys in the course of the novel tend to cause upheaval.

- The limited family life of the Brontës in their isolated Yorkshire community, and the extent to which they were outsiders, is reflected directly in the claustrophobic world of *Wuthering Heights*.

- Wild personalities and locations were evidently part of Brontë's childhood and are significant in the fictional world of the novel. Brontë's brother, the infamously wild Branwell, for example, is reflected in Heathcliff.

- Family deaths, particularly of young people, form a significant element within both Brontë's life and *Wuthering Heights*.

- In Brontë's life and in the novel, mother figures are significant by their absence.

- Children are left to face the world alone and vulnerable.

- Unmarried girls are either left to face the world alone or placed under the protection of ineffective male guardians in a society stacked against them.

- Brontë's inability to live comfortably as a conventional lady is reflected in the characters of Cathy and Catherine.

- The location of the Brontë family home links to the final image of the novel and its symbolic force.

Wild personalities and locations were part of Brontë's childhood.

Cultural and social context – religion

The novel's treatment of religion is astonishing, given that Brontë was the daughter of a clergyman. It concentrates on the dark, complex and disturbing motivations of a set of characters locked in a cycle of irreligious violence and brutalism. Heathcliff in particular is a profoundly dark character, arguably a psychopath. While operating within conventional religious terms and with established ideas of good and evil, the novel pushes the boundaries of violence and sexuality to (and beyond) the limits of Victorian tolerance.

CRITICAL VIEW

Bloom (1998) writes of the dark side of spirituality:

These excluded areas … often retain a strong peripheral or inverted relationship with orthodox religion [and] embrace the practices usually termed occult. In such systems there is much more direct relationship with the invisible realms.

This sheds an interesting light on the role of conventional religion in the Gothic genre, which often seems to reject religious orthodoxy and the establishment. How far, in fact, does *Wuthering Heights* reject conventional religious views and how far does it reinforce them?

Hypocrisy and sin

Religion emerges as a key issue from early in the novel. Heathcliff's servant Joseph is a religious hypocrite. Brontë compares him to the Pharisees – Jewish religious teachers renowned for their adherence to the letter rather than the spirit of God's law. They are a byword for hypocrisy. Jesus referred to them as hypocrites, and once as 'you brood of vipers' (Matthew 12: 34). Joseph accuses Catherine of dabbling with arcane powers and the dark arts, an accusation which she jokingly enjoys. This paves the way for later appearances of the supernatural and arcane in the novel. Mr Lockwood's dream of Jabez Branderham establishes an air of nightmarish religious mania in the novel. The preacher's sermon focuses on the issue of forgiveness of sin, which is highly significant as the novel portrays so much sin and so little ability to forgive it. Transgression and trespass are central to the novel.

Heaven

Brontë also uses religious contexts when Cathy explains to Nelly how she 'should be extremely miserable' in heaven. She goes on to recount a vivid dream in which she has gone to heaven. However:

> 'heaven did not seem to be my home; and I broke my heart with weeping to come back to earth; and the angels were so angry that they flung me out, into the middle of the heath on the top of Wuthering Heights; where I woke sobbing for joy.'

Cathy here can be compared to Lucifer in Milton's *Paradise Lost* who is also ejected from Heaven. The comfort she finds in her dream at being at the Heights makes it seem a place divorced from heaven, with its brutal violence, hatred and dissent. This passage is important as both Cathy and Heathcliff try to establish an alternative heaven with each other. This is reflected towards the end of the novel, when Heathcliff fearlessly rejects Christian tenets. Heaven for him is reunion with Cathy, even though throughout his life this relationship has caused him such great torment. Brontë maintains the possibility that for Cathy and Heathcliff an alternative, non-Christian heaven may exist.

Prayer

Prayer is another important religious idea in the novel. Isabella recounts Heathcliff's satanic and blasphemous prayers of revenge. When she compares his prayers to those of the Methodists – a non-conformist Christian sect noted for their strict dedication – she illustrates his fervency. Prayers also play a part elsewhere in *Wuthering Heights*. When Heathcliff almost kills Hareton after visiting Cathy's grave he calls Joseph in and forces him to pray. The prayer seems oddly out of place in the midst of such violence. The image of Joseph on his knees in the middle of a pool of blood is striking. Isabella's laughter at the 'phraseology' of the prayer suggests that religion is misplaced, and how little it is heeded.

Vengeance

When she is recounting her terrible experiences at the Heights, Isabella invokes the Old Testament maxim of revenge (an eye for an eye) in defence of her position (see Deuteronomy 19: 20–21). In her own words, she wishes to 'reduce [Heathcliff] to my level'. This attitude contrasts strikingly with the view expressed by Nelly Dean, who adopts the truly Christian view in the face of hatred and violence. She alludes to the biblical principle that vengeance belongs to God and that humans should not seek retribution of their own for wrongs they have suffered. It is only through revenge that Isabella feels her suffering can be atoned for. It is interesting to compare this with Mr Lockwood's dream of Jabez Branderham and Christ's doctrine of forgiveness.

Abysses and mountains

Abysses and mountains are highly significant, especially in the Gothic genre. Mountains, towers and spires are often representations of 'masculine' activity and dominance, while dark caverns, pits and cellars represent 'feminine' passivity and weakness. Freudian, feminist and Marxist readings of the text often rely on these ideas as symbols of motivation, gender and power.

Mountains and abysses also have significant religious overtones. The abyss is an image of hell and damnation. The book of Revelation, among others, refers to the abyss into which Satan or the Beast is cast, and from which he will emerge as the Antichrist. In a Freudian reading the dark places represent subconscious, repressed desire – places where 'unacceptable' wishes can flourish. In the biblical context caverns and abysses are places of dark activity, active threat and power. Mountains are also significant in the Bible. They are holy places in the stories of Noah, when the Ark lands on Mount Ararat, the giving of the Law to Moses on Mount Sinai, the defeat of the prophets of Baal by Elijah on Mount Carmel, the story of the Transfiguration, the Sermon on the Mount, and the temptation of Christ on the mountain by Satan. In all of these stories and more, mountains are places of revelation. High places are also sometimes attached to evil, however; the prophets of Baal frequently used 'high places' to make their sacrifices to their god.

In *Wuthering Heights*, there are two 'high' locations. Catherine, unbeknown to her father and Nelly, journeys to Penistone Crags, where she first encounters Heathcliff. The dominating physical presence of the Crags powerfully lures Catherine, attracting her into destructive relationships with Linton and Heathcliff. The Heights, as its name makes clear, is also a 'high' location. It contrasts to the relatively low-lying Thrushcross Grange.

Taking it further

Read Deuteronomy 19: 20–21; Deuteronomy 32: 35 and Romans 12: 19–21.

Context

Brontë's father was a clergyman and she grew up familiar with Christian teaching. Read the following passages in the Bible about mountains and abysses:

- Revelation 20: 1-8
- Exodus 19-20
- 1 Kings 18
- Matthew 17: 1-13

TASK

Think about: power, revelation, passivity, weakness. How does Brontë relate these to high and low places?

Literary context

Gothic

Gothic is a loosely defined form, but nevertheless has a number of typical features. The following list covers the most common:

- wild landscapes
- ruined or grotesque buildings
- religious settings/religious concepts
- sensibility
- excess and extremity
- the supernatural
- imagery of darkness, shadow, decay
- the exotic and oriental
- horror and terror
- isolation and loneliness
- sanity and insanity
- sex and sexuality
- use of multiple narrators
- crime, lawlessness and abuse
- absolute power
- the devilish and arcane
- the outsider.

Build critical skills

Identify examples of each of these Gothic devices in *Wuthering Heights*.

Roots of the Gothic

The roots of the Gothic precede the classic works of the eighteenth and nineteenth centuries. The following list suggests a number of the key authors and movements that influenced the rise of the Gothic form, and which can be compared to *Wuthering Heights*:

- Elizabethan and Jacobean tragedy — supernatural, vice, corruption, imprisonment, brutality, sexuality
- Graveyard poetry — Blair, Young, Parnell; focus on decay and death
- William Blake — suspicion of organised religion; the essential coexistence of opposites
- The Romantics — notably Wordsworth, Coleridge and de Quincey; focus on the natural world and its relation to the state of humankind
- The novel of sensibility — excess of emotion and extremity
- Milton — religion; the battle between good and evil
- Medieval Gothic — the grotesque, gargoyles

Manifestations of Gothic

Below is a broad outline of the various mainstream forms of Gothic and some of its key figures:

- Romance (Ann Radcliffe, Charlotte Dacre, Clara Reeve)
- Ghost story (Henry James, M.R. James, Susan Hill)
- Horror (Edgar Allan Poe, James Herbert, Stephen King)
- Fantasy (J.R.R. Tolkien, Mervyn Peake)

- Mystery/adventure (Sir Arthur Conan Doyle, Henry Rider Haggard, H.G. Wells)
- Sensation (Wilkie Collins, Mary Elizabeth Braddon)
- Decadence (Robert Louis Stevenson, Oscar Wilde, Bram Stoker)
- Arcane (H.P. Lovecraft)

Dualisms within Gothic

Gothic texts often use opposition and division. The genre depends upon uncertainty and conflict. These are also key issues in *Wuthering Heights*, which deals with questions of moral, social, religious and personal doubt. Brontë presents a world where distinctions are blurred and where confusion often reigns. Brontë's presentation of these issues is never straightforward. The ambiguity we feel in relation to the central issues of the novel leads to a deep ambivalence in our attitude towards the characters and scenarios portrayed.

Gothic … depends upon uncertainty and conflict.

Gothic images

Many artists have worked in what may be termed a Gothic style. William Blake and Goya are two of the best-known examples. Goya once wrote: 'Fantasy abandoned by reason produces impossible monsters.' The following pictures are examples of the Gothic style:

▲ *The Nightmare* (1781) by Henry Fuseli

73

Taking it further ▶

The 'Fiction' section within 'Taking it further' on page 108 of this guide suggests further reading. Try reading a selection of texts by these authors and see how they add to your understanding of Gothic as a form.

◥ Goya – *The Sleep of Reason Produces Monsters* (*El Sueño de la Razon Produce Monstruos*). Davenport-Hines (1998) refers to this painting as 'Perhaps the most important single image for the historian of the Gothic'.

◥ William Blake – *The Good and Evil Angels*

◥ Henry Fuseli – *The Nightmare*

◥ Caspar David Friedrich – *The Cross in the Mountains*.

Brontë often creates great visual impact through her words. As you read, take time to visualise the scenes she paints for you.

Build critical skills

Take each of these key divisions (a dichotomy is a sharply defined division). How do you see each one operating in *Wuthering Heights*?

- Good/evil
- Male/female
- Innocence/guilt
- Reality/fantasy
- Natural/supernatural
- Freedom/imprisonment
- Human/inhuman
- Internal/external
- Natural/unnatural
- High/low
- Moral/immoral/amoral
- Light/dark

Romanticism

Another significant literary context for *Wuthering Heights* is Romanticism. Generally speaking Romanticism was a late-eighteenth-century/early-nineteenth-century movement in music, art and literature. Because of the nature of the Romantic temperament it is hard to define. However, it emphasises individual sensibility, the boundless, the indefinite and the visionary.

Because of its prioritisation of the individual and the relationship of humanity with numinous (spiritual) concepts like the visionary and the sublime, a fuller definition is difficult. *The Oxford Companion to English Literature*, however, offers the following:

> *In the most abstract terms, Romanticism may be regarded as the triumph of the values of imaginative spontaneity, visionary originality, wonder, and emotional self-expression over the classical standards of order, restraint, proportion, and objectivity … Its name derives from romance, the literary form in which desires and dreams prevail over everyday realities.*

Build critical skills

Four key ideas of the French philosopher Jean-Jacques Rousseau were taken up by the Romantics:

- Increasing separation of Man from Nature
- Increasing unhappiness and loss of virtue
- Society imposes restraints on the individual
- Humans have an innate sense of justice and virtue that leads to principled action

How do the ideas in the above context box relate to the major concerns and events of *Wuthering Heights*?

Romanticism was a profound, quasi-spiritual reaction to the confined and orderly rationalism of the **Enlightenment**. The Romantics asserted the importance of individual feeling, warning against the incursion of hard 'reason'. Wordsworth decried what he called the 'meddling intellect' and looked for meaning in the human heart, arguing that science, with its tendency to dissect the natural world and its endless desire to define and categorise, was the negation of poetry. In Germany the philosopher Immanuel Kant encouraged many Romantics to elevate nature, seeing in it a reflection of the soul, the sublime and the divine. Meanwhile, in France, Rousseau asserted the rights of the individual and the need for greater corporate responsibility. In England, political thinkers like Carlyle, Godwin and Wollstonecraft wrote a new socio-political agenda. These revolutionary ideas led to a period of enormous social and political upheaval (including European and American revolutions).

The **Enlightenment** was a period marked by increasing empiricism and scientific rigour and as a result, an increased questioning of conventional religious beliefs.

Taking it further ▶

Emily Brontë wrote only one novel. However, she did write a significant number of poems, many of which reflect thematically and linguistically upon *Wuthering Heights*. Use the first lines of these poems (below) to search for them on the internet:

- ▶ 'Sleep brings no joy to me'
- ▶ 'Cold in the earth — and the deep snow piled above thee'
- ▶ 'How beautiful the earth is still'
- ▶ 'I'll not weep that thou art going to leave me'

How do these poems seem to relate to *Wuthering Heights*? Useful ideas might be: death, sleeplessness, graveyards, storms, sadness, hopelessness, coldness, desperation, gloom, separation, isolation, darkness, spirituality, sentiment/emotion.

Wuthering Heights and *King Lear*

Brontë invokes this parallel herself. Like the hapless King Lear in his daughter's house, Mr Lockwood finds himself imprisoned and maltreated by the servants at Wuthering Heights:

> …then, hatless and trembling with wrath, I ordered the miscreants to let me out – on their peril to keep me one minute longer – with several incoherent threats of retaliation that, in their indefinite depth of virulency, smacked of *King Lear*. (p. 17)

The Heights, like Shakespeare's play, is a place of senseless, self-perpetuating violence and self-interest.

Themes

The two texts share several major themes:

- senseless and extreme brutality
- sanity and insanity
- familial jealousy
- individuals and society.

Location

Both *King Lear* and *Wuthering Heights* use barren heath or moorland settings to symbolise threat, emptiness and infertility. Wild locations are used to represent the wild passions and brutal emotions that drive the action. Wilderness proves to be a place of understanding, however, where characters come face to face with the frequently unpleasant realities of their lives. Through his insanity and privations on the heath, Lear understands what he should truly value, and reconciliation with his faithful daughter Cordelia becomes possible. Similarly, through the 'madness' of their conflict, the Earnshaws and Lintons (in Catherine and Hareton) eventually achieve union, untainted by ambition or revenge.

Storms

Storms play a significant symbolic role in both texts. A fearsome storm breaks after Lear has been thrown out of his daughters' houses. The storm forces Lear to reconsider his position and his actions. In the course of *Wuthering Heights* there are a number of significant storms:

- Mr Lockwood is trapped at the Heights by a snow storm.
- A furious storm breaks on the night that Heathcliff leaves the Grange.
- Heathcliff's return is greeted by a heavy and storm-laden atmosphere.

These storms symbolise and externalise the inner turmoil of the characters, familial division, insanity, anger, hatred, brutality and social upheaval.

Names

There are two important coincidences of name between Shakespeare's play and Brontë's novel:

- Edgar – in both texts Edgar is well meaning, loyal and frequently naïve, and is caught up in a whirlwind of passionate events beyond his control. In *King Lear*, Edgar is abused by his illegitimate brother Edmund; in *Wuthering Heights*, Edgar becomes the victim of the outcast Heathcliff. Both Edmund and Heathcliff are stigmatised and mistreated because of their questionable births, and as a result develop into violent, vengeful and unprincipled men.

- Heathcliff – this name combines two of the most important locations in *King Lear*: the heath where Lear finally recognises his foolishness and the cliff where the blinded Gloucester realises he has been wrong to trust Edmund. Both are key places of personal awakening in the play. The heath (moors) and the cliff (Penistone Crags/the Heights) are also highly significant places of encounter in *Wuthering Heights*. Heathcliff himself forces others to a true and painful understanding of themselves. He is like a barren landscape, as Cathy points out. Nobody emerges unscathed from their encounters with him.

Taking it further ▷

Read *King Lear* and explore the important comparisons further. You might also try developing a similar set of comparisons with *Hamlet*.

▲ Paul Shelley as Gloucester and William Postlethwaite as Edgar, King Lear at the Theatre Royal Bath, 2013

Critical contexts

Critical voices

The following worked examples draw on criticism relating to Gothic fiction, and apply this to *Wuthering Heights*. The examples show how critical comment can be used in order to gain a fuller understanding of how Brontë has adopted the form and demonstrate a range of the critical ways in which readers might 'receive' the novel. A secondary aim of this section is, by targeting a number of critical points of view, to provide a basis for thought and discussion when relating *Wuthering Heights* to your wider reading.

The subversive

> *Gothic was the archaic, the pagan, that which was prior to, or resisted the establishment of, civilised values and a well-regulated society.*
>
> (Punter, 1996)

Note Punter's emphasis upon the 'external' and subversive nature of Gothic which, he suggests, lies at the edges of the acceptable; hence it is linked with a historically remote time, or with the religiously suspect (witchcraft, the pagan, non-Protestant religion), the exotic and the foreign. Even where the action of the texts is firmly located in England, setting and events often indicate values and demands that lie outside the bounds of the conventional and the acceptable.

The bizarre and unfamiliar

> *Gothic was chaotic ... ornate and convoluted ... excess and exaggeration, the product of the wild and uncivilised.*
>
> (Punter, 1996)

The excessive, the bizarre and the unfamiliar are all significant here. They suggest a disturbingly unpredictable and threatening world. Violent action and extreme emotion, often incompletely explained, and the use of wild locations, create a disconcerting lack of security. The fictional world of *Wuthering Heights* abounds in chaos. The confused relations between the Linton and Earnshaw households, the multiple interweaving narratives, and the nature of the characters' lives are all chaotic.

The Gothic borderlands

> *Gothic works, it is often objected, are not fully achieved works: they are fragmentary, inconsistent, jagged ... If Gothic works 'do not come out right', this is because they deal in psychological areas which themselves do not come out right, they deal in those structures of the mind which are compounded with repression rather than with the*

Build critical skills

In what ways do you think *Wuthering Heights* is a subversive novel?

purified material to which realism claims access … And it is here that we come to the crux of the matter: Gothic writers work – consciously or unconsciously – on the fringe of the acceptable, for it is on this borderland that fear resides. In the best works, the two sides of the border are grafted onto each other.

(Punter, 1996)

In this extract, Punter identifies the importance of uncertainty and incompleteness. The form itself reflects its content and concerns; the Gothic does not deal in neat and orderly situations, and therefore the works themselves are frequently neither neat nor orderly. Confusion of action and motive are significant. Heathcliff, Cathy and many of the other characters in *Wuthering Heights* are perfect examples of this. At the heart of the novel and its many dilemmas and cruelties lies characters' peculiar inability to understand their own motivations, needs, desires and actions. Relationships within the closed communities of the Heights and the Grange, as well as with the wider world, often prove complex and confusing. Characters are frequently paired and associated with each other in the reader's consciousness, the result of which is that the distinctions between them become deliberately and increasingly uncertain as the novel progresses.

Blurring the edges

The Gothic was and remained the dimension of the imperfectly perceived.

(Punter, 1996)

Many Gothic narratives, including *Wuthering Heights*, gain considerable effect from blurring the edges of the narrative – liminality. Transitions between narrators and the varying perspectives they offer on events, along with the uncertainties engendered by paralleling the characters, create in us a sense of uncertainty and unease. This is a studied and deliberate effect, reflecting accurately the profound doubt and confusion underlying the form itself.

The forbidden

It is in its concern with paranoia, with barbarism and with taboo that the vital effort of Gothic fiction resides: these are the aspects of the terrifying to which the Gothic constantly and hauntedly returns.

(Punter, 1996)

Wuthering Heights, like many other Gothic texts, deals with the forbidden and the dangers of pursuing the forbidden. This raises questions about the reader's morality and pleasure in reading and enjoying these texts.

> **Build critical skills**
>
> Make a list of all the forbidden activities and opinions you can think of in the novel. What dangers do these taboos lead characters into?

Distortion and exaggeration

The Gothic is a distorting lens, a magnifying lens; but the shapes which we see through it have nonetheless a reality which cannot be apprehended in any other way.

(Punter, 1996)

Here Punter suggests that the distortions and exaggerations of Gothic serve a necessary purpose in helping writers (and readers) to approach the unapproachable. The form serves a social function, allowing writers to explore things that might otherwise lurk dangerously undiscovered. Brontë employs distorted characters, motivations, relationships and families to highlight the dangers of social exclusion, rejection, violence and revenge.

Realism and symbolism

Gothic fiction thus finds itself operating between two structural poles. On the one hand, because it rejects the account which realism gives of the world, it seeks to express truth through the use of other modes and genres – poetic prose, the recapture of tragedy, expressionistic writing, the revival of legend, the formation of quasi-myths – in order to demonstrate that the individual's involvement with the world is not merely linear but is composed of moments with resonances and depths which can only be captured through the disruptive power of extensive metaphor and symbolism.

(Punter, 1996)

> **Build critical skills**
>
> What major symbols does Brontë make use of in *Wuthering Heights*? What do these symbols represent?

Brontë creates a fragile balance between the realistic and the symbolic. The relationship between the two is essential – a preponderance of either element leads to an imbalance and a consequent reduction in the impact of the writing and its ability to instil fear and uncertainty.

Terror and horror

Terror and Horror are so far opposite, that the first expands the soul and awakens the faculties to a higher degree of life; the other contracts, freezes and nearly annihilates them. I apprehend that neither Shakespeare nor Milton by their fictions, nor Mr Burke by his reasoning, anywhere looked to positive horror as a source of the sublime, though they all agree that terror is a very high one; and where lies the great difference between terror and horror, but in uncertainty and obscurity, that accompany the first, respecting the dreaded evil?

(Ann Radcliffe, from 'On the Supernatural in Poetry', 1816)

The difference between terror and horror is a key distinction as far as Radcliffe is concerned. Terror has morally elevating and uplifting potential, as opposed to the morally and spiritually enervating impact of horror. Devendra Varma was one of the first critics to seize on this distinction, characterising the difference between terror and horror as the difference between 'awful apprehension and sickening realisation'. Robert Hume has also embraced this distinction, although in slightly different terms; he argues that the horror novel replaces the ambiguous physical details of the terror novel with a more disturbing set of moral and psychological ambiguities. Robert L. Platzner (1971), while not challenging entirely the difference between terror and horror, notes where the edges blur. He refers specifically to the writings of Ann Radcliffe, but the application is more general: 'It appears that far from never crossing the boundary between terror and horror, Mrs Radcliffe compulsively places her heroine in situations of overwhelming anxiety in which a gradual shift from terror to horror is inescapable.' This links directly to the situations of many of Brontë's characters in *Wuthering Heights*, who find themselves repeatedly subjected to cruelty, brutality and fear.

Using literary theory

Three worked examples follow, demonstrating how concepts drawn from literary theory can be applied to *Wuthering Heights*. It is important to look at a wider range of theories and to consider how these can all feed into your reading of the text. Knowledge of a range of theoretical positions will enable you to develop your abilities as an effective reader.

Sigmund Freud

Sigmund Freud (1856–1939), a psychoanalyst, formulated his theories in a series of books, *The Interpretation of Dreams* being the most well-known. His work led to many interesting developments in the literary world, including the rise of the psychoanalytic school of literary criticism, which has been highly influential. He is most famous for propounding the concepts of the Oedipus complex (an innate sexual attraction to the parent of the opposite sex), the **death wish**, a focus upon the phallus as a symbol and its corollary, **penis envy**, as well as the formulation of the divisions within the human psyche.

death wish - the desire for annihilation

penis envy - female sense of loss at not having male genitalia

Childhood

Freud's concentration on infancy as the basis for subsequent psychological development is highly significant. Throughout the novel, Nelly Dean focuses on the progress of the children of the Earnshaw and Linton households. Considerable importance is attached to the varied home environments within which the children grow up. Cathy is changed forever by her stay at the Grange with the Lintons, and the differences between Heathcliff and Edgar are invoked repeatedly. Heathcliff's uncertain parentage and early childhood, and his hard upbringing in the Earnshaw household twist his character and mark him forever. In his turn, he deliberately terrorises Linton, and brutalises Hareton. Standing *in loco parentis* after Hindley's death, he calculatedly fails in his parental duties of nurture and affection, leading to a continuation of the cycle of revenge within the novel.

Sexuality

Freud believed that sexuality, repressed or otherwise, lies at the root of human behaviour. In *Wuthering Heights* the most powerful example of this is the relationship between Heathcliff and Cathy, and its contrast with the relationship between Cathy and Edgar. The animal-like ferocity of Cathy and Heathcliff's physical contact, teetering always on the brink of the desire to inflict physical pain, brings violence into romance in a daring and highly provocative way. Nelly Dean is unable to account for such passion. Cathy certainly sees her personality and her very being as totally embodied in Heathcliff: 'I am Heathcliff!' Interestingly, the relationship remains unconsummated until their bizarre union in the grave. By contrast, the relationship between Cathy and Edgar is an apparently passionless affair, lacking the fire of her contact with Heathcliff, although it is, nevertheless, consummated, leading to the birth of Catherine.

The concept of Oedipal relationships is also important. Linton Heathcliff, for example, seeks to re-establish, under his father's guidance, the relationship that existed between Heathcliff and Isabella. The convergence of the houses of Earnshaw and Linton also points towards a close-knit, almost incestuous web of relationships.

The self

The divided self is a further crucial element of Freud's theory. He identifies a three-way division of the human psyche into the 'id' (appetite-driven desires), the 'ego' (conscious sense of 'self' and awareness of others) and the 'super-ego' (sense of morality, sometimes seen as conscience). In *Wuthering Heights*, Brontë explores the warring elements of the self. She presents the divided and deeply flawed nature of Heathcliff and many of the other characters by externalising their internal conflict through the doubling of characters. The most overt example of this is the 'division' (or multiplication) of Cathy into Cathy Linton/Earnshaw/Heathcliff.

The death wish

Freud saw the death wish as a powerful psychological drive, based on a continuing desire to return to the womb. This can be linked to Brontë's use of dark, enclosed spaces (coffins, the garret where Mr Lockwood sleeps and the enclosed wooden bed are like nightmarish wombs). Cathy dies, wishing vindictively that her death may inflict suffering and haunting on Heathcliff locking him into a pursuit to the death of an image of his hoped-for reunion with her. On a number of occasions he expresses the wish that his sufferings could be ended by death.

Karl Marx

Karl Marx (1818–83) is best known for *Das Kapital*—an outspoken attack on the capitalist system. His concept of 'historical materialism' has been highly influential in the Marxist school of literary criticism, which seeks to understand literature as a form of material production that participates in and illuminates the processes of history.

There are many perceived social or political 'messages' within *Wuthering Heights*. The novel hinges upon social inclusion/exclusion. The text highlights particularly the dangers of social isolation and the consequences of domestic tyranny. Brontë also looks at the issue of female inheritance rights and the threats posed to women within a patriarchal society.

Wuthering Heights was written in a time of political uncertainty between the two electoral Reform Acts. This was a period of social and class upheaval in England, and a time when the rights of women were beginning to be considered.

Readers of *Wuthering Heights* could consider how the plot, characters and settings reflect the concept of class struggle, either by inclusion or omission. The novel is keenly aware of issues of class; Brontë makes clear the threat posed to the status quo by the socially suspect Heathcliff. As an adoptive son of the Earnshaws, he enjoys the status and rights of a prosperous yeoman farmer, but remains distinctly separate from them. He is a thorn in the flesh of the established landowners. The novel also considers female rights of inheritance; Edgar seeks to protect Catherine from the predatory intentions of Heathcliff who, after Linton's death, stands to inherit the Grange.

A final key concept here is the way that class renders characters alienated from society. Mr Lockwood is isolated socially; Heathcliff fights for, but never establishes, his right to be accepted; the Heights and the Grange remain isolated and have little contact with the social world of Gimmerton and beyond.

Feminism

Feminism is a modern tradition of literary criticism devoted to the defence of women's writing or of female characters within a predominantly male literary establishment. A number of ideas central to the feminist point of view are highly relevant to *Wuthering Heights*.

Wuthering Heights challenges many of the typical perceptions of women in Gothic; far from being silent and passive, women are active competitors in a violent domestic world. Cathy, Catherine, Isabella and Nelly Dean are all strong women who refuse to remain silent in the face of their maltreatment, and Mrs Earnshaw, although present in the text only briefly, gives every impression of being a dominant figure in her household. The women in the novel are no more helpless when confronted with the power of Heathcliff than are many of the male characters.

'Nor are the women in the novel the product of male fantasy. Cathy, Catherine and Isabella are all beauties, but do not conform to traditional models of propriety, and certainly do not take on the extreme and extended passivity characteristic of so many Gothic females.

Wuthering Heights deals extensively with the issue of domestic violence, which is frequently (though not exclusively) directed at women. It highlights too the problem of inequality within inheritance law, and the difficulties and dangers to which this often subjected women. Even though many of the women in the novel are strong characters, they are still largely obliged to live under the 'protection' of males.

Taking it further ▶

Look at the representation of women in a number of the other works of fiction suggested in the 'Fiction' section of 'Taking it further' on page 108. How do Brontë's women compare and contrast with them?

Working with the text

Assessment Objectives and skills

> **A01**   Articulate informed, personal and creative responses to literary texts, using associated concepts and terminology, and coherent, accurate written expression.

To do well with AO1 you need to write fluently, structuring your essay carefully, guiding your reader clearly through your line of argument and using the sophisticated vocabulary, including critical terminology, which is appropriate to an A-level essay. You will need to use frequent embedded quotations to give evidence of close, detailed knowledge, and you should demonstrate familiarity with the whole text. Remember, however, that quotation is not the only way of referring to the text – paraphrasing and alluding to relevant events are also perfectly valid methods of showing that you have a detailed knowledge of the text and can be more effective than awkwardly trying to incorporate quotations that do not quite work. The ideal is to produce a well written academic essay employing appropriate discourse markers to create the sense of a shaped argument; it should use sophisticated terminology at times while remaining clear and cohesive.

> **A02**   Analyse ways in which meanings are shaped in literary texts.

Strong students do not work only on a lexical level, but also write well on the generic and structural elements of the novel, so it is useful to start by analysing those larger elements of narrative organisation before considering Brontë's use of language in *Wuthering Heights*. If 'form is meaning', what are the implications of categorising the novel as a Gothic text, a ghostly tale, a romance or a Victorian novel? How does form take on different meanings in each case? The narrative is structured in a very distinctive way, as further explored in the 'Form, structure and language' section of this book, and there has been much debate about the ways in which Brontë creates connections and distances between her narrators and their parallel narratives. Then again, in order to discuss language in detail you will need to quote from the text, analyse your quotations and use them to illuminate your argument. Moreover, since you will at times need to make points about larger generic and organisational features of the novel which are much too long to quote, being able to reference effectively is just as important as mastering the art of the embedded quotation. You could practise writing in analytical sentences, including a brief quotation or close reference, a definition or description of the feature you intend to analyse, and an explanation of how this feature has been used and an evaluation of its effectiveness.

AO3	Demonstrate understanding of the significance and influence of the contexts in which literary texts are written and received.

To access AO3 successfully you need to think about how contexts of production, reception, literature, culture, biography, geography, society, history, genre and intertextuality can affect texts. Place the novel at the heart of the web of contextual factors which you feel have had the most impact upon it; examiners want to see a sense of contextual alertness woven seamlessly into the fabric of your essay rather than a clumsy bolted-on website rehash or some recycled history notes. Show you understand that literary works encode representations of the cultural, moral, religious, racial and political values of the society from which they emerged, and that over time attitudes and ideas change until the views they reflect are no longer widely shared.

AO4	Explore connections across literary texts.

If your examination board requires you to compare and contrast one or more other texts with *Wuthering Heights* you must try to find specific points of comparison, rather than merely generalising. You will find it easier to make connections between texts (of any kind) if you try to balance them as you write; remember also that connections are not only about finding similarities – differences are just as interesting. Above all, consider how the comparison illuminates each text; some connections will be thematic, others generic or stylistic.

AO5	Explore literary texts informed by different interpretations.

For AO5, you should refer to the opinions of critics and remain alert to aspects of the novel which are open to interpretation. Your job is to measure your own interpretation of the text against those of other readers. As a text that has generated widely differing responses, *Wuthering Heights* lends itself readily to the range of interpretations which have been noted in the 'Critical contexts' section of this book (see p. 78). Try to convey an awareness of multiple readings as well as an understanding that the meaning of a literary text is dependent as much upon what readers bring to it as what Brontë might have meant by it. Using modal verb phrases such as 'may be seen as', 'might be interpreted as' or 'could be represented as' shows you know that different readers interpret texts in different ways at different times. The key word here is plurality; there is no single meaning or one right answer. Relish getting your teeth into the views of published critics to push forward your own argument, but always keep in mind that meanings in texts are shifting and unstable, not fixed and permanent.

Summary

Overall, the hallmarks of a successful A-level essay that hits all five AOs include:

- a clear introduction which orientates the reader and outlines your main argument
- a coherent and conceptualised argument which relates to the question title
- confident movement around the text rather than a relentless chronological trawl through it
- apt and effective quotations or references adapted to make sense within the context of your own sentence
- a range of effective points about Brontë's narrative methods
- a strong and personally engaged awareness of how a text can be interpreted by different readers and audiences in different ways at different times
- a sense that you are prepared to take on a good range of critical and theoretical perspectives
- a conclusion which effectively summarises and consolidates your response and relates it back to your essay title.

Building Skills 1: Structuring your writing

This Building Skills section focuses upon organising your written responses to convey your ideas as clearly and effectively as possible: the 'how' of your writing as opposed to the 'what'. More often than not, if your knowledge and understanding of *Wuthering Heights* is sound, a disappointing mark or grade will be down to one of two common mistakes: misreading the question or failing to organise your response economically and effectively. In an examination you'll be lucky if you can demonstrate 5 per cent of what you know about *Wuthering Heights*; luckily, if it's the right 5 per cent, that's all you need to gain full marks.

Understanding your examination

It's important to prepare for the specific type of task your examination body sets with regard to *Wuthering Heights*. You'll know whether you are studying the novel as part of a **non-examined assessment unit** (for coursework) or as an **Open Book examination set text** – in which case you will have a clean copy of the text available to you in the exam, or **Closed Book**, in which case you won't. The format of your assessment has major implications for the way you organise your response and dictates the depth and detail required to achieve a top band mark.

Open Book

Both AQA A 'Love Through the Ages' and Edexcel 'Women and Society' are Open Book exams. In an Open Book exam when you have a copy of *Wuthering Heights* on the desk in front of you, there can be no possible excuse for failing to quote relevantly and accurately. To gain a high mark, you are expected to focus in detail on specific passages. Remember, too, that you must not refer to any supporting material such as the Introduction Notes accompanying the text. If an examiner suspects that you have been lifting chunks of unacknowledged material from such a source, they will refer your paper to the examining body for possible plagiarism.

Non-examined assessment (NEA)

Writing about *Wuthering Heights* within a non-examined assessment unit (coursework) context poses a very different set of challenges. Your essay must be wholly and consistently relevant to the title selected; there's no excuse for going off track if you or your teacher mapped out the parameters of your chosen topic in the first place. Remember that all NEA tasks require independence and you will be expected to explore how different critical and theoretical interpretations or ideas can be applied to the text.

Step 1: Planning and beginning: locate the debate

A very common type of exam question invites you to open up a debate about the text by using various trigger words and phrases such as **'consider the view that …'**, **'some readers think that …'** or **'how far do you agree with this view?'** Exam questions never offer a view that makes no sense at all or one so blindingly obvious all anyone can do is agree with it; there will always be a genuine interpretation at stake. Similarly many NEA tasks are written to include a stated view to help give some shape to your writing, so logically your introduction needs to address the terms of this debate and sketch the outlines of how you intend to move the argument forward to orientate the reader. Therefore you really do need to plan before you begin to write.

Undertaking a lively debate about some of the ways in which *Wuthering Heights* has been and can be interpreted is the DNA of your essay. Any stated view in an examination question is designed to open up critical conversations, not shut them down.

Plan your answer by collecting together points for and against the given view. Aim to see a stated opinion as an interesting way of focusing upon a key facet of *Wuthering Heights*, like the following student.

Student A

This student is addressing the view that Mr Lockwood is 'an uninspiring narrator who tells a good tale in spite of himself' and exploring Brontë's use of him in *Wuthering Heights* in response to the following question modelled on the sort you will find on **Edexcel's** 'Women and Society' theme:

Compare the ways in which the writers of your two chosen texts make use of different narrative voices. You must relate your discussion to relevant contextual factors.

Emily Brontë in Wuthering Heights and Mary Shelley in Frankenstein both choose to use multiple narrators. The tales they tell are complex, and at their hearts lay the recognition that the same events can often be seen in different ways. The narrators that both writers employ are central in shaping readers' views. Mr Lockwood is a romantic idealist who has travelled to Yorkshire to experience the beauty of the moors. It is hard, as the quotation suggests, to see him as 'an uninspiring narrator'. He may be naïve, but he is also perceptive — accurately judging Heathcliff to be a man who will 'love and hate, equally under cover' — and has a well-developed sense of irony (e.g. his initial observation that Heathcliff is a 'capital fellow!'), which shows us he is not without humour. Brontë is at pains to show us that Mr Lockwood is gentlemanly and polite, which sets him radically apart from Heathcliff and the other characters. He serves an essential function: as an interested and observant (if often bemused) 'foreigner', his narrative provides readers with a suitably distanced perspective on the dark and labyrinthine Yorkshire world he has entered. His narrative provides a contextualizing frame for the vigorous, though not necessarily reliable account of Nelly Dean.

In Frankenstein Mary Shelley employs three main narrators. Like Mr Lockwood, Captain Walton is a frame narrator. Unlike in Brontë's tale, however, the connection between Walton's narrative and that of the other narrators — Frankenstein and his creature — is strong. As an explorer ambitious to make his name by discovering a new trade route, Walton naturally relates to the hapless Frankenstein and his tale of over-reaching ambition. The 'monster' Frankenstein creates is also encountered by Walton and could easily become a part of his future. Frankenstein's narrative emerges naturally from Walton's as the creature's in turn emerges naturally from Frankenstein's. Whilst the narratives of Mr Lockwood and Nelly Dean complement each other, the narratives of Walton, Frankenstein and the creature are organically related.

Examiner's commentary

This student:

- Challenges the proposition that Mr Lockwood is an uninspiring narrator and uses it as a basis to introduce his narrative and the narratives of the other narrators in the two novels.

- Makes effective use of brief quotations, incorporating these neatly within their own writing.

- Comments critically on how Mr Lockwood as narrator compares to Nelly Dean.

- Explores the natural connection between Mr Lockwood as outsider and the reader, who shares his outsider's view.

- Expresses a confident personal sense of different ways in which narrative functions in the two novels, setting up an effective platform for further discussion.

- Establishes a clear sense of how Mr Lockwood's and Captain Walton's frame narratives connect in different ways to their respective novels.

If the rest of the essay reached this level of performance, it is likely it would be on course to achieve a notional grade A.

Step 2: Developing and linking: go with the flow

An essay is a very specific type of formal writing that requires an appropriate discourse structure. In the main body of your writing, you need to thread your developing argument through each paragraph consistently and logically, referring back to the terms established by the question itself, rephrasing and reframing as you go. It can be challenging to sustain the flow of your essay and keep firmly on track, but here are some techniques to help you:

- Ensure your essay doesn't disintegrate into a series of disconnected building blocks by creating a neat and stable bridge between one paragraph and the next.

- Use discourse markers – linking words and phrases like 'on the other hand', 'however', 'although' and 'moreover' – to hold the individual paragraphs of your essay together and signpost the connections between different sections of your overarching argument.

- Having set out an idea in Paragraph A, in Paragraph B you might need to support it by providing a further example; if so, signal this to the reader with a phrase such as '***Moreover*** *the significance of religious imagery can also be seen when …*'.

▼ To change direction and challenge an idea begun in Paragraph A by acknowledging that it is open to interpretation, you could begin Paragraph B with something like *'**On the other hand**, this view of the novel could be challenged by a feminist critic ...'*.

▼ Another typical paragraph-to-paragraph link is when you want to show that the original idea doesn't give the full picture. Here you could modify your original point with something like the passage from the following extract: *'**Although** it is possible to see Nelly Dean's narrative as a well-informed overview, it is important to remember that she is also a significant participant in many of the novel's events, and as such her narrative needs to be read with some caution.'*

Student B

Like Student A, this student is addressing the Edexcel-style question on narrative voices.

Brontë draws on contrasts. The difference between Mr Lockwood and Heathcliff is established immediately at the beginning of the novel when Mr Lockwood observes that 'Mr Heathcliff and I are such a suitable pair to divide the desolation between us'. The contrast between Mr Lockwood's gentility and the brutality of Heathcliff serve an important function. Mr Lockwood is a true gentleman, and as such gives us a means of reading Heathcliff who is also described as a gentleman. Remember also that, apart from Heathcliff, Mr Lockwood is the only true outsider to come into the milieu of the novel, and as such provides an important external view to which readers can relate. This is quite different to the effects Mary Shelley achieves in Frankenstein. Whilst in some ways comparable in its use of multiple narrative voices, Shelley's novel, rather than establishing the distances between the narrative voices of Captain Walton, Victor Frankenstein and the creature, explores the ways in which their narrative perspectives and voices more and more meld into one until in many ways their voices become indistinguishable.

Both Mr Lockwood and Captain Walton are somehow separated from the major events of the tales they recount. They do not, however, function solely as narrators; they are also active agents. Mr Lockwood recounts vividly and effectively the opening section of the novel and creates an almost palpable air of brooding menace. For example, the skulking dogs of the opening chapter seem to reflect the curious assembly of residents at the Heights and suggest imminent threat. The plethora of household items is used to capture the tawdry, dark and oppressive nature of Heathcliff's house. These display Mr Lockwood's lively and precise facility with words, as do his vivid recounts of his dreams of Jabez Branderham and the ghostly visitation of Cathy. All of these function effectively on their own, but Brontë also uses them to pave the way efficiently for Nelly's explanatory narrative. Similarly, Captain Walton's letters 'frame' the central tale of Frankenstein and his creature. In this case, however, we are constantly made aware not of the differences but the tight similarities between Walton and his counterpart, Frankenstein. Both are prepared to go to extremes in their pursuit of (forbidden?) knowledge, and as such both are involved in active encounters with the creature, whose own narrative has a profound impact on the hearts of both men.

Unlike Captain Walton, whose close affinity with Frankenstein enables him to empathise with Victor and his dilemma, Mr Lockwood is at times confused by what he experiences and this emerges in his narrative. This is hardly surprising, and is part of his effectiveness as we too enter the bizarre social world of the novel. We share, for example, his uncertainty about the history of the house, the families and the relationship between the Heights and the Grange. His role as narrator is, in a sense, to raise the questions that Nelly will go on to 'answer' in her narrative. She is an insider, thoroughly familiar with life at the Heights and the Grange. Although it is possible to see Nelly Dean's narrative as a well-informed overview, however, it is important to remember that she is also a significant participant in many of the novel's events, and as such her narrative needs to be read with some caution. Feminist critics might well be interested to explore the differences between Mr Lockwood's and Nelly's narratives from a gender perspective.

Examiner's commentary

This student:

- ▼ Expresses their ideas with clarity – their use of language is efficient and precise.
- ▼ Creates very good cohesion between paragraphs by clearly connecting the stages of their argument.
- ▼ Uses well-chosen discourse markers – 'the juxtaposition of', 'remember also that', 'if … at times' and 'for example' – to signpost the flow of their ideas.

> ⬩ Deals in a balanced and effective way with both texts, using understanding of core 'connecting' issues as a basis for discussion of texts.
>
> ⬩ Makes a very neat paragraph-to-paragraph link to indicate how Mr Lockwood's narrative realtes to but also differs from Captain Walton's.
>
> ⬩ Identifies that narratives are 'gendered' and that Mr Lockwood's and Nelly's narratives might be affected by this. The point, however, is undeveloped.
>
> **If the rest of the essay reached this level of performance, it is likely the student would be on course to achieve a notional grade B.**

Step 3: Concluding: seal the deal

As you bring your writing to a close, you need to capture and clarify your response to the given view and make a relatively swift and elegant exit. Keep your final paragraph short and sweet. Now is not the time to introduce any new points – but equally, don't just reword everything you have already said. Neat potential closers include:

⬩ Looping the last paragraph back to something you mentioned in your introduction.

⬩ Reflecting on your key points in order to reach a balanced overview.

⬩ Ending with a punchy quotation that leaves the reader thinking.

⬩ Discussing the contextual implications of the topic you have debated.

⬩ Reversing expectations to end on an interesting alternative view.

⬩ Stating why you think the main issue, theme or character under discussion is so central to the novel.

⬩ Mentioning how different audiences over time might have responded to the topic you have been debating.

Student C

Like Students A and B, this student is also responding to the question about narrative voice.

Mr Lockwood is one of a number of narrators in the novel. He provides what is known as a frame narrative – a tale that surrounds the main events of the novel. Brontë might be using his position as an outsider to reflect the position of the reader who shares his uncertainty and discomfort as he enters the unpredictable and violent society of this remote community. This is rather different from Nelly Dean's narrative which is based on extensive 'inside' knowledge. This demonstrates how authors can use narrative point of view to create different effects. Although Mr Lockwood is part of the novel he is only really involved in the later parts of the tale. His narrative encloses Nelly's, which in turn encloses other narrative elements told by other characters.

Examiner's commentary

This student:

- ◤ Keeps their conclusion short, but offers nothing apart from a simple restatement of the key issues relating to Mr Lockwood.

- ◤ Begins to clarify their argument about the ways in which different narrative voices exist in the novel, but does not really actively debate the original task focus.

- ◤ Does not take the tried-and-tested route of partially accepting the stated view.

- ◤ Loosely relates Mr Lockwood to the events of the novel and to Nelly Dean's narrative, but draws no meaningful conclusion about this.

- ◤ Includes simple feature-spotting with the statement that 'He provides a frame narrative' and offers a brief analysis of how or why the novelist does this.

- ◤ Does not use reference to the other text to create meaningful connections or contrasts.

If the rest of the essay reached this level of performance, it is likely it would be on course to achieve a notional grade C or D.

Building Skills 2: Analysing texts in detail

Having worked through the previous Building Skills section on structuring your writing, this section of the guide contains a range of annotated extracts from students' responses to *Wuthering Heights*. The next few pages will enable you to assess the extent to which these students have successfully demonstrated their writing skills and mastery of the Assessment Objectives to provide you with an index by which to measure your own skills progress. Each extract comes with a commentary to help you identify what each student is doing well and/or what changes they would need to make to their writing to target a higher grade.

The main focus here is on the ways in which you can successfully include within your own well-structured writing clear and appropriate references to both *Wuthering Heights* itself and the ways in which other readers have responded to the novel. In an examination, of course, the 'other reading' you need to refer to consistently may be expressed in the question itself, but you should always look for opportunities to incorporate reference to other critical and theoretical points of view. In an NEA unit, you will have more time and space to deal with varied interpretations of the texts you most want to work with.

Analysis in examination tasks

Student A

This student is answering a sample examination task similar to the types of question set on the **AQA Specification A AS** paper which puts forward a specific view. The question, which is clearly designed to open up a debate, is:

'By focusing on emotion and passion, writers often make romance the most memorable aspect of their work.'

By comparing two prose texts, explore the extent to which you agree with this statement.

Note that for purposes of this guide, only extracts dealing in detail with *Wuthering Heights* have been included.

Wuthering Heights is full of violent shifts and contrasting emotions, and romance in the tale is no different. In her relationships with Heathcliff and Edgar, Brontë presents Cathy as a mass of mixed emotions and 'constantly varying caprices'. She is almost 'unearthly' and lethargic at one moment, full of passionate energy and 'wild vindictiveness' the next. Her physical state is testament to the destructive nature of her passions which seem to take her to the brink of insanity. Like Cathy, Heathcliff is a mass of contradictory emotions (impatience, grief, despair, self-pity, remorse, resentment and surprising restraint by turns). He seems to be controlled by his passions rather than remaining in control of himself. Edgar on the other hand is proper, gentlemanly, reserved and quietly determined. Brontë achieves a powerful and memorable impact on the reader in her representation of the intense triangular relationship between these characters. The passions and emotions she explores, however, are not those one would readily associate with romance. As Nelly Dean observes, the story of Cathy, Edgar and Heathcliff draws a 'strange and fearful picture' of the lengths and depths to which passion can drive people.

Romance and passion (of sorts) are also a central feature of Angela Carter's set of tales, *The Bloody Chamber*. Like Brontë, Carter uses elements of the gothic genre to explore the very fringes of romance. In her afterword to *Fireworks*, Carter attributes the gothic what she calls a 'singular moral function'. This function, she goes on to explain is to provoke unease. Both Carter and Brontë create such unease by seasoning their representations of romance with elements and behaviours that force us to challenge and to question what we thought we knew. By employing binary opposites such as tenderness and cruelty, love and hate, freedom and constraint, they establish boundaries around which to explore what we understand by romance and love. For all that *Wuthering Heights* and *The Bloody Chamber* might appear to eschew conventional boundaries and limitations, they derive their true power not from rejecting boundaries, but by insisting on them. Acts of deviance and transgression relentlessly and disturbingly test out precisely what is and is not acceptable.

'The Bloody Chamber', for instance, begins with a young girl on the sexually charged borderline between two lives as she leaves childhood and enters on marriage; she departs 'the white, enclosed quietude of my mother's apartment' for 'the unguessable country of marriage'. The castle in the same tale is on the boundary of the sea and land, separated by a causeway clear only at low tide, which serves to emphasise her isolation and vulnerability. This 'sea-girt, pinnacle domain that lay... beyond the grasp of my imagination', like the Heights, is a place that is almost beyond the realms of the possible. As such, it is a suitably liminal space where the girl (like Catherine, Cathy and Isabella) is 'both the inmate and the mistress' and where Carter can explore the boundary between innocence and corruption.

Other types of contrast are also significant. Brontë makes liberal use of images of animals/humans, imprisonment/freedom, life/death, heaven/hell in her representations of romance and strange love. Cathy and Heathcliff's love defines (and breaks) itself upon these oppositions and appears far from romance: it is brutal, tragic, passionate and undeniably powerful, but it is also very far from conventional. Heathcliff is a deeply troubling version of the Byronic hero, and Cathy is an equally unconventional heroine of romance. Love and the desire to inflict pain, to relate and to revenge are inextricably linked in a mutually destructive passion. The binary opposition of attraction and repulsion is at the heart of their relationship and the novel as a whole. A similar situation seems to be replaying itself in the relationships between Catherine, Linton and Hareton.

In *The Bloody Chamber*, Carter deploys a similar set of devices. Masks and skin are frequently used to represent boundaries or barriers, representing attempts to cover up in both a protective and a deceptive sense. The mask worn by the husband in 'The Bloody Chamber' conceals his face and the truth of his personality from his young bride. His thick beard — an almost bestial touch — serves a similar function. When he returns to the island after his intended journey to New York, the misting over of his eyes acts as a further and even more sinister form of masking. In order to try to penetrate these 'masks', the young wife, left alone in the castle whilst her husband goes on an unexpected business trip, seeks out the forbidden room to understand the 'real man' behind the façade.

Like Brontë, whose presentation of Heathcliff's and Cathy's romance abounds with animal imagery (Heathcliff is compared amongst other things to a wolf, a serpent, a lion and a dog), Carter also explores the extent to which human passions are 'animal'. In 'The Tiger's Bride', the beast is 'not much different from any other man, although he wears a mask with a man's face painted most beautifully on it.' This connective-transgressive blurring of the human and animal worlds is, perhaps, at its most strident and complete in 'Wolf-Alice' of whom Carter tells us: 'Nothing about her is human except that she is not a wolf; it is as if the fur she thought she wore has melted into her skin and become part of it, although it does not exist'. Such dislocations of the natural world create deep uncertainty about the nature of love and romance in both *Wuthering Heights* and *The Bloody Chamber*.

Examiner's commentary

This student:

- ⬏ Refers back to the terms of the question frequently, reframing the key ideas of emotion and passion along the way.
- ⬏ Makes very effective use of embedded quotation assimilated fluently into their own writing.
- ⬏ Takes on the premise of the question by suggesting how both Brontë and Carter have produced highly unconventional 'romance' — it seems likely that this opinion would be developed further to provide the spine of the essay.
- ⬏ Uses appropriate connectives like 'on the other hand' and 'similar' and 'however' to signal the developing stages of the argument.

- ◤ Forges a very clear link between the two texts. It is clear that this is not a surface comparison of the two texts but emerges from particular and well-defined literary contexts relating to gothic.

- ◤ Uses careful phrasing 'seems to be' and 'are not necessarily' together with the subtle verb 'suggests' to flag up awareness that textual meanings are unfixed and always open to question.

- ◤ Demonstrates very good AO2 awareness around structure by referring to binary opposition.

If the rest of the examination answer reached this level of performance, it is likely it would be on course to achieve a notional grade A.

Analysis in non-examined assessments

Student A

Note that there is a difference with regard to NEA assessment for Edexcel and AQA A. Candidates following Edexcel **are permitted** to write NEA responses on any texts listed in the specification provided they are not also being examined on the same text. **This is not the case** for students following AQA A where the specification clearly states: 'Texts listed in the A-level core set text and comparative set text lists in Sections 4.1 and 4.2 cannot be studied for non-exam assessment.'

This student is writing for their NEA assessment in response to the following task:

Compare the ways in which the writers of your two chosen texts make use of different voices. You must relate your discussion to relevant contextual factors.

In both Emily Brontë's 'Wuthering Heights' and Virginia Woolf's novel 'Mrs Dalloway', the writers employ the technique of narrative voice in order to give considerably marginalised characters a voice, providing them with a sense of liberation and freedom that they do not receive in their respective restrictive societies. In 'Wuthering Heights', narrative voice is portrayed through the two characters of Nelly, whose narration is mainly oral and Mr Lockwood, whose journal actually forms the frame of the novel, whereas in 'Mrs Dalloway', the narrator is omniscient, although there are continual changes in the points of view throughout the novel.

In 'Mrs Dalloway', the notion of being told a story from the narrator's point of view is extremely important to the narrative as a whole. Due to the omniscient, third person narrator, the narrative does not permit the readers to ever gain the full truth of the novel. Thus the readers are completely reliant on the few bits of information that we receive from the narrator to form a judgement on the characters, which we subconsciously assume to be reality, yet this is a fickle assumption. This narrative style prevents the readers from forming a subjective view of the characters. The character of Peter is undermined from the start of the novel, and the reader receives the least information about him. It is important to highlight that the denial of information is deliberate by Woolf, for the purpose of highlighting the mystery and secrecy concerning Daisy. In contrast, in 'Wuthering Heights', the narrative voice is used explicitly for the purpose of enabling the readers to form objective opinions concerning the characters as we receive insights not only to the plot, but also the characters themselves. This allows the readers to focus on the narrative plot, and much less on the characters themselves in order for the narrative to express the truth, as this portrayal of reality is not discredited by judgements made by the readers.

It is also important to highlight that in 'Mrs Dalloway', Woolf chooses to follow the narrative structure of the stream of consciousness in order to mimic the theme of wandering thoughts. This creates a sense of intimacy between both the readers and the characters, as the readers feel as though we have a greater access to the 'true' character despite the constant changing points of view. This stream of consciousness also provides the characters with a sense of freedom; they can express themselves fully without being hindered. Whereas in 'Wuthering Heights', Brontë chooses a non-linear narrative structure, providing the readers with both flashbacks and flash-forwards, in order to encompass the readers in the plot, adding to the sense of the meandering of thoughts.

In Brontë's 'Wuthering Heights' the narrative voice is not used to give the characters freedom. In fact it can be argued that the characters are restricted by the narrative form as it denies the voice of Nelly, as the purpose of the text is not to give the author a voice, but to give the text a voice, telling the story without any involvement from the narrator. In spite of this it can also be argued that while Nelly has no obvious voice within the novel, the fact that she is a character within her narrative does give her a voice as she participates in the story. It is also important to highlight the importance of the narrative voice of Mr Lockwood. The narrative form of the diary allows the readers to see the events of the plot from a first-hand perspective, thus creating a sense of closeness between the author and the readers. Similar to Nelly, this narrative form gives Mr Lockwood who is limited in the fact that he is an outsider, a sense of liberation as he is free to express himself openly. This is also echoed in Woolf's 'Mrs Dalloway'.

Examiner's commentary

Note how this student:

- ◥ Constructs a controlled argument.
- ◥ Embeds examples effectively.
- ◥ Makes effective use of literary terminology and concepts.
- ◥ Shows a clear sense of how meanings are shaped in texts and analyses elements of the writers' craft.
- ◥ However, shows limited awareness of contextual factors.
- ◥ Treats the texts as separate entities and does not really 'connect' them.

If the rest of this NEA response continued at this level of performance, it is likely it would be on course to achieve a notional grade C or D.

Extended commentaries

Lockwood visits Wuthering Heights (Vol. 1, Chapter 2)

As so often in *Wuthering Heights*, the weather plays a central part in this passage. Coming early in the novel, Brontë's presentation of the Heights has an important influence on the ways in which we perceive the farm and its occupants. The 'misty and cold' afternoon on which Mr Lockwood makes his visit is prohibitive, and were it not for the 'infernal dust' the maid is creating in his study at the Grange, it is clear that he would not have ventured out. The use of the word 'infernal' here may simply be a mild expletive, but may also be suggestive of the hellish world of the Heights that Mr Lockwood is about to encounter. The weather continues to be important as the passage progresses. The 'heath and mud' Mr Lockwood crosses on his four mile walk to the Heights (note how distant the two houses are one from the other) are replaced when he reaches the Heights by 'earth … hard with a black frost'. The change in the nature of the land and the air temperature capture the change in atmosphere that comes with the Heights. The rock hard earth and the freezing air seem apt representations for the harshness of the house, its forbidding nature and the reception Mr Lockwood receives. The assertion that the frost is 'black' makes the environment seem even more threatening, and when the hardness and coldness of the ground are supplemented by the 'first feathery flakes of a snow-shower' which soon begins to 'drive thickly', our sense that this is a formidable and harsh place is heightened.

Faced with a locked gate, a locked door and Joseph's obstinate unwillingness to help, Mr Lockwood mentally curses its inhabitants for their 'churlish inhospitality'. Once he does gain access to the house, however, the outward harshness of the environment is seemingly belied by the 'huge, warm, cheerful apartment' he is shown into, which 'glowed delightfully in the radiance of an immense fire, compounded of coal, peat, and wood'. The apparent warmth of the place is supplemented by the promise of 'a plentiful evening meal'. Brontë contrasts the 'plentiful meal' with the inadequate dining arrangements Mr Lockwood found at the Grange, the warmth and red glow of the fire at the Heights with the coldness and monochrome black (frost) and white (snow) of the outside world, and the apparent promise of life in the imagined 'obscure cushion full of something like cats' with the realisation that it is in fact 'a heap of dead rabbits'. These contrasts neatly prepare us for the extremes and the internal conflicts that are to be so characteristic of the novel as a whole, and appearing here they serve to create a sense of unease. If he expects conventional hospitality, however, Mr Lockwood is to be disappointed. The 'missis', when he meets her does not convey the anticipated invitation to be seated by the fire, but instead 'remained motionless and mute'. We gain a sense that there is a far more oppressive power at work at the Heights. The figure of the Master, first introduced by Joseph, looms over this passage, and it is evident that Catherine is afraid to act. As much is again suggested by Joseph when he tells Mr Lockwood: 'There's nobbut t' missis; and shoo'll not oppen 't an ye mak' yer flaysome dins till neeght.' Why, we wonder, should this be the case?

This passage also interestingly provides us with an insight into the voice of Mr Lockwood and suggests the nature of his relationship to the tale he recounts. First of all, it is useful to note the journal form that he employs. The introductory 'Yesterday afternoon' serves to create the immediacy of a journal and reminds us that although the events the novel recounts may spread back into a dark and murky past, the frame story and Mr Lockwood's visit to the Heights are very much of the here and now. We gain the sense of a man who is used to refinement (he is easily driven away from the Grange by the dusty work of the housemaid) and regular in his habits. These routines he does not like to have changed, but he is, nevertheless, unable to assert his own will. Although he is the master of the Grange, the housekeeper refuses to give in to his instructions about when he wishes to dine, and Mr Lockwood has to content himself with a rather disgruntled parenthesis in his journal: '(N.B. – I dine between twelve and one o'clock; the housekeeper, a matronly lady, taken as a fixture along with the house, could not, or would not, comprehend my request that I might be served at five)'. This suggests a man who tends to be of particular, though not forceful, opinions; a man who retains a certain mannered detachment from the world of the Grange and the Heights.

The end of the novel (Vol. 2, Chapter 20)

In the final pages of the novel, weather again proves to be significant. Nelly Dean comments on the fact that the weather 'was very wet: indeed, it poured down till day-dawn'. It is this that alerts her to the fact that something is wrong prior to her discovery of Heathcliff's dead body. It is not only the wetness of the conditions that is significant here, but the fact that the window has been left open allowing the water to pour into the house. Throughout *Wuthering Heights* windows, doors and gates are significant; they represent points of connection; points of entry and exit; and now, as we learn of the departure of Heathcliff from this life, the image is again significant.

When Nelly first enters the room, she can scarcely believe him dead. Firstly she concentrates on his eyes, which 'met mine so keen and fierce' and 'then he seemed to smile'. It is as if even in death Heathcliff retains the power to live on. It is not until she observes that he is 'perfectly still' and that he has not bled in spite of the cut on his arm from the flapping of the shutter that she accepts 'he was dead and stark'. The ambiguity surrounding life and death established here is significant as we approach the end of the novel. Heathcliff's body seems resistant to death. Mr Kenneth, the doctor, is 'perplexed to pronounce of what disorder the master died', as if his death cannot be defined by a conventional diagnosis. Then, when Nelly tries to shut Heathcliff's eyes, she cannot; not even death seems capable of extinguishing his 'frightful, life-like gaze of exultation' and the sneer of 'his parted lips and sharp white teeth'. Joseph strikes the note of the supernatural when he observes that '"Th' divil's harried off his soul"'. The story of the young boy who claims to have encountered Heathcliff and a woman 'yonder, under t' nab' and the accounts of the 'country folks' who 'would swear on the Bible that he walks', suggest that the spirits of Heathcliff and Cathy live on. Nelly Dean's assertion that the dead (Heathcliff and Cathy) 'are afraid of nothing' – note the use of the present tense verb here – and her belief that 'Together, they would brave Satan and all his legions' demonstrates her conviction that they continue to exert their dark influence over the Heights and its locale. It is, therefore, fitting and not surprising that Hareton and Catherine have decided to make their married home at the Grange.

Our enduring memories of the world of *Wuthering Heights*, however, do not lie with the future, they reside in the past and perhaps for that reason, Brontë ends the novel with Mr Lockwood's ruminations on the deceased. The final image of the novel is neither of the Heights nor of the Grange, but of the wild and lonely graveyard where Cathy, Edgar and Heathcliff have been buried, if not exactly laid to rest. The language of the novel's concluding paragraphs creates an appropriate sense of ambiguity and uncertainty. The 'decay' of the kirk contrasts with the beauty of the natural environment; the death associated with the graveyard contrasts with the life of the fluttering moths and the harebells; the serenity of the time and place as embodied in 'that quiet earth' are undermined by the 'unquiet slumbers' of the dead; and the threatened 'coming autumn storms' provide a sense of imminent threat to counterbalance 'that benign sky'. Liminal states have been significant throughout the novel, and Brontë leaves her narrator, Mr Lockwood, intensely alive to such states as the novel comes to a close.

Perhaps the most striking image, however, is the final picture of the graves of Heatchcliff, Cathy and Edgar all arranged in a row. Cathy is appropriately placed between the two men who have been so important and painful in her life. Brontë uses simple yet powerful descriptions of the graves to capture something of the nature of her protagonists and of the tale she has told. Edgar – the most conventional – is buried entirely within the confines of the graveyard and his grave is green – 'harmonised by the turf'. Cathy, as befits her marginal state and the contradictions of her life, is buried straddling sanctified and unsanctified ground. Appropriately her grave is 'grey', a colour representative of doubt and uncertainty. Heathcliff's grave is entirely in the unholy ground of the heath and is 'bare' as if unable to sustain any kind of colour or life.

Brontë, through her narrator Mr Lockwood, leaves us not with answers, but with uncertainty. While Hareton and Cathy move to start their new lives at the Grange with all the potential to forge a new beginning, Edgar, Cathy and Heathcliff remain a dominant and potent force as the novel concludes. Mr Lockwood might wonder 'how anyone could ever imagine unquiet slumbers for the sleepers in that quiet earth', but the rapid decay of the kirk and the threat of 'coming autumn storms' along with Nelly's threatening prognostications about the continued existence of the dead leave us with more than a little doubt.

Top ten quotations

Before studying this section, you should identify your own 'top ten' quotations
– those phrases or sentences that seem to capture a key theme or aspect of
the text most aptly and memorably – and clearly identify what it is about your
choices that makes each one so significant. No two readers of *Wuthering
Heights* will select exactly the same set and it will be well worth discussing (and
perhaps even having to defend) your choices with the other students in
your class.

When you have done this, look carefully at the following list of top ten
quotations and consider the possible significance of each one within the novel.
How might each be used in an essay response to support your exploration
of various elements or readings of *Wuthering Heights*? Consider what these
quotations tell us about Brontë's ideas, themes and methods as well as how far
they may contribute to various potential ways of interpreting the text.

Wuthering Heights is the name of Mr Heathcliff's dwelling, 'Wuthering' being a
significant provincial adjective, descriptive of the atmospheric tumult to which
its station is exposed in stormy weather. (p. 4)

1

> ◥ The name of Heathcliff's house encapsulates what we should
> expect of Heathcliff – tumult, exposure and storms. The quotation
> exemplifies Brontë's use of the natural world to symbolise the
> emotional world of her characters. Mr Lockwood's observations about
> Wuthering Heights at the beginning of the novel indicate quite how
> isolated a place it is. This is clearly symbolic, distancing the cruel,
> barbarous and excessive events of the text from the everyday world;
> it also emphasises the defencelessness of the novel's victims, who
> are kept far from any external source of aid. The loneliness of the
> situation makes it inevitable that Mr Lockwood, as a newcomer, will
> be perceived as an interloper, an outsider. A final use of this quotation
> could be to reflect upon the character of Mr Lockwood, with the
> slightly pejorative use of the adjective 'provincial'.

We don't in general take to foreigners here, Mr Lockwood, unless they take to us
first. (p. 46)

2

> ◥ Nelly Dean's observation captures the confined and claustrophobic
> social world of Wuthering Heights, Thrushcross Grange and their
> surrounding community. Gimmerton, the nearest town, seems a long
> way away and the inhabitants of these isolated homes live in a world
> apart. She emphasises the inward looking, suspicious and narrow-
> minded social mileu of the novel. There is something aggressively

exclusive in what she says, and it is clear that it is a place where compromise is not to be expected. As an outsider, Mr Lockwood has to win the favour of the locals, not the other way around. The novel deals harshly with 'foreigners'. Heathcliff's ethnicity remains something of a mystery and he is never really accepted into the world of the Heights and the Grange. Others who take themselves away from this social circle, such as Isabella and Linton, have great difficulties in reintegrating. Note, too, the second half of this quotation – the onus is firmly placed on outsiders to accept and fit in with the ways of life at the Grange and the Heights.

3 My great miseries in this world have been Heathcliff's miseries, and I watched and felt each from the beginning: my great thought in living is himself. If all else perished, and he remained, I should still continue to be; and if all else remained, and he were annihilated, the universe would turn to a mighty stranger: I should not seem a part of it. My love for Linton is like the foliage in the woods: time will change it, I'm well aware, as winter changes the trees. My love for Heathcliff resembles the eternal rocks beneath: a source of little visible delight, but necessary. Nelly, I am Heathcliff! He's always, always in my mind: not as a pleasure, any more than I am always a pleasure to myself, but as my own being. (p. 82)

⌐ Here Cathy tries to capture for Nelly Dean her feelings for Edgar and Heathcliff. She has already agreed at this point to marry Edgar as she feels that to marry Heathcliff would 'degrade' her. Brontë uses this passage and its images of the natural world to capture the contrast between the two men and to pave the way for much of the future unhappiness of the novel. Catherine's transitory and mutable feelings for Edgar (the foliage) contrast with her enduring feelings for Heathcliff (the 'eternal rocks'). However, Brontë uses the richness of her language to suggest more than this simple dichotomy. Her use of the word 'winter' implies hard times to come. We could also comment on her choice of images – the leaves though short-lived, are a thing of beauty as compared to the rocks which give 'little visible delight' – to represent the two men. Also note the definitive conclusion – 'I am Heathcliff!' which Brontë uses to capture their indivisible union.

4 'Tell her what Heathcliff is – an unreclaimed creature, without refinement – without cultivation; an arid wilderness of furze and whinstone.' (p. 102)

⌐ Here Cathy gives her view of Heathcliff when Isabella is thinking of marrying him. This is another fine example of Brontë's use of the natural world to present character. The quotation seeks to capture Heathcliff's impenetrable nature. This, of course, remains a mystery throughout the novel. However, the quotation does raise some important issues with regard to Heathcliff. The use of the word 'creature' with its animal overtones is important, capturing here as elsewhere something of his wildness, romance and unpredictability. When she observes that he is 'unreclaimed' and 'without refinement – without cultivation', Brontë illustrates again Heathcliff's rugged and socially unacceptable nature. The words in themselves, however, suggest that under different circumstances he would have been capable of refinement and cultivation. This encourages us to see him as victim as well as victimiser. The comparison to the wild moors – a dry, infertile and hostile place – adds to our sense of him as living outside of civilised – urban? – values.

'Is Mr Heathcliff a man? If so, is he mad? And if not, is he a devil?' (p. 136)

5

▼ In a letter to Nelly Dean, Isabella expresses her desperation. The quotation could be used in any question dealing with Heathcliff's character to explore the range of emotions he evokes within us. The impact of these three short and straightforward sentences is considerable as they encapsulate such a variety of response. As we saw in the previous quotation, Brontë often compares Heathcliff to animals. Here the same sentiment is differently framed. We are not asked to question whether he is an animal, we are asked to question whether he is a man. The implication may be that he is less than a man, but it may also be that he is more than a man. As much is suggested by the third sentence here, where we entertain the possibility that he is a supernatural being. Brontë repeatedly uses supernatural comparisons for Heathcliff in the novel. It is clear that we cannot consider either Heathcliff or his behaviour as normal. The second sentence questions his sanity. The steady escalation (or descent) through these three questions – from humanity, to madness, to the satanic has an inevitable and powerful rhythm.

'… I assure you, a tiger, or a venomous serpent could not rouse terror in me equal to that which he wakens.' (p. 144)

6

▼ This passage, from a letter from Isabella to Nelly Dean, again uses animals to represent the character of Heathcliff. First of all, notice the wild and dangerous natures of the animals Isabella chooses for her comparisons – the tiger and the snake. These are fierce and untameable creatures, but they are exotic too, and this adds a further dimension to Heathcliff. For all that he is wild and dangerous, he is also something unusual, precious and unknown. Remember how he is found on the streets of Liverpool and how his ethnicity and provenance remain mysterious. The animals here represent something of Heathcliff's own potentially exotic and mysterious background. The serpent carries satanic overtones. We note that both the tiger and snake are considered preferable to and less dangerous than Heathcliff, which emphasises the deadly nature of the man and the fear he strikes into the hearts of the other characters in the novel.

7 '... far rather would I be condemned to a perpetual dwelling in the infernal regions, than even for one night abide beneath the roof of Wuthering Heights again.' (p. 183)

⊣ Speaking to Nelly, Isabella illustrates the nightmarish quality of life at Wuthering Heights. Isabella is obviously not an unbiased observer and she speaks from the bitter pain of her experience. Like the previous two quotations, it emerges from the novel's train of hellish imagery. While Heathcliff is not specifically named, it is apparent that he is the major focus of this remark, although the house, as we see early in the novel, is in itself a dark and fearsome place. The true dreadfulness of the Heights is emphasised by the opinion expressed that eternal damnation is better than a single night there. This quotation could also be used when discussing Brontë's use of excess within the novel.

8 Catherine's face was just like the landscape – shadows and sunshine flitting over it, in rapid succession; but the shadows rested longer and the sunshine was more transient, and her poor little heart reproached itself for even that passing forgetfulness of its cares. (p. 266)

⊣ This quotation provides a beautiful and poetic example of Brontë's use of imagery from the natural world. Her word-painting vividly captures Catherine's momentary escape from emotional trauma as she faces the death of Edgar and her coming exposure to Heathcliff. The motions of the clouds and the sun reflect the dancing of terrible experience (shadows) and hope (sunshine) across Catherine's features. These 'shadows' and 'sunshine' may be either external – the influence of Heathcliff, Edgar and her traumatic lived experience – or internal, and Brontë uses these to represent Catherine's deeply scarred psyche. The words 'flitting' and 'rapid succession' demonstrate the complexity of Catherine's emotions and their speed and unpredictability. Brontë suggests something open, honest and selfless in Catherine's nature when she observes how she reproaches herself for taking pleasure in nature at the expense of thinking about her father's situation. This quotation could also be used in a discussion of Brontë's presentation of nature, to illustrate that it can be beautiful as well as a threatening force.

Catherine spoke with a kind of dreary triumph: she seemed to have made up her mind to enter into the spirit of her future family, and draw pleasure from the griefs of her enemies. (p. 288)

9

> Here Nelly Dean demonstrates the infectious disease of hatred and psychological brutality at the Heights and the Grange. Catherine has just delivered a passionate speech to Heathcliff, telling him that nobody loves him and that nobody will grieve his death. Notice, however, Nelly's use of the phrase 'dreary triumph'; through this Brontë suggests something resigned and even regretful in Catherine's attitude. This implies that it is alien to Catherine's nature, but we are also informed that Catherine has consciously adopted behaviours that seem contrary to her temperament (she has 'made up her mind'). When Catherine allows herself to succumb to the vindictive atmosphere spreading from the warped natures of Heathcliff and Linton, Brontë demonstrates how evil pervades the novel. We may feel that Catherine is a victim — most of the characters in the novel are victims to some extent — but we also have to acknowledge that she does not have to choose this as a course of action.

I tried to close his eyes — to extinguish, if possible, that frightful, life-like gaze of exultation, before anyone else beheld it. They would not shut — they seemed to sneer at my attempts, and his parted lips, and sharp, white teeth sneered too! (p. 335)

10

> Even in death, Heathcliff remains recalcitrant. His corpse seems alive and exultant, as if in achieving death Heathcliff has obtained all that he wants and needs. He is a force that is not to be extinguished; he seems more than mortal. The sharp, dog-like teeth (taking us full circle back to the lurking, threatening dogs of the beginning of the novel) are a defiant reminder of his life and inevitably suggest something of the vampire. This powerful depiction of Heathcliff in death ensures that his image remains seared on our minds and goes with us as the novel comes to a close.

Taking it further

References

Booth, W.C. (1961) *The Rhetoric of Fiction* (Chicago: University of Chicago Press)

Fraser, J. (1965) 'The Name of Action: Nelly Dean and Wuthering Heights' *Nineteenth-Century Fiction*, Vol. 20, No. 3

van Ghent, D. (1953) *The English Novel: Form and Function* (New York: Rinehart)

Hafley, J, (1958) 'The Villain in Wuthering Heights' *Nineteenth-Century Fiction*, Vol. 13, No. 3

Haggerty, G. (1989) *Gothic Fiction/Gothic Form* (Pennsylvania State University Press)

Herman, D., Jahn M. and Ryan, M. (2005) *Routledge Encyclopedia of Narrative Theory* (London: Routledge)

McKibben, R.C. (1960) 'The Image of the Book in Wuthering Heights' *Nineteenth-Century Fiction*, Vol. 15

Oates, J.C. (1983) 'The Magnanimity of Wuthering Heights' *Critical Inquiry*

Platzner, R.L. (1971) '"Gothic versus Romantic": A Rejoinder' *PMLA*, Vol. 86

Todorov, T. (1977) *The Poetics of Prose*. Translated by Richard Howard (Wiley-Blackwell)

Worth, G.J. 'Emily Brontë's Mr Lockwood' *Nineteenth-Century Fiction*, Vol. 12, No. 4

Fiction

Austen, J. (1818) *Northanger Abbey*

Collins, W. (1860) *The Woman in White*

Conan Doyle, Sir A. (1901) *The Hound of the Baskervilles*

le Fanu, S. (1864) *Uncle Silas*

Gaskell, E. *Gothic Tales* (first published as a collection in 2000)

Godwin, W. (1794) *Caleb Williams, or Things as They Are*

Hill, S. (1983) *The Woman in Black*, (1992) *The Mist in the Mirror*

James, H. (1898) *The Turn of the Screw*

James, M.R. (1931) *Casting the Runes and Other Stories*

Lewis, M. (1796) *The Monk*

Maturin, C. (1820) *Melmoth the Wanderer*

Poe, E.A. (1839) *The Fall of the House of Usher*

Radcliffe, A. (1792) *The Romance of the Forest*

Shelley, M. (1818) *Frankenstein*

Stoker, B. (1897) *Dracula*

Walpole, H. (1764) *The Castle of Otranto*

Poetry

Blake, W. (1893) *The Four Zoas*

Byron, (1813) *The Giaour*

Coleridge, S.T. (1798) *The Rime of the Ancient Mariner*

Keats, J. (1819) 'La Belle Dame sans Merci'

Poe, E.A. (1845) 'The Raven'

Young, E. (1742) The *Complaint, or, Night-thoughts on Life, Death and Immortality*

Criticism

- Bloom, C. (ed.) (1998) *Gothic Horror: A Reader's Guide from Poe to King and Beyond* (Macmillan)
  – A classic exploration of the use of horror in literature.

- Davenport-Hines, R. (1998) *Gothic: Four Hundred Years of Excess, Horror, Evil and Ruin* (Fourth Estate)
  – Looks at the historic sweep of Gothic fiction, particularly interestingly looking at the idea of excess.

- Gilbert, S. and Gubar, S. (1979) *The Madwoman in the Attic: The Woman Writer and the Nineteenth-Century Literary Imagination* (Yale University Press)
  – A central work of feminist literary criticism looking at the role of women in nineteenth-century literature.

- Kilgour, M. (1995) *The Rise of the Gothic Novel* (Routledge)
  – Interestingly explores some of the formal properties of Gothic fiction.

- Kranzler, L. (2000) Introduction to Elizabeth Gaskell's Gothic Tales (Penguin)
  – A succinct introduction to Gothic and some of its major preoccupations.

- Punter, D. (1996) *The Literature of Terror* (Longman)
  – The definitive guide to Gothic literature and its sources.

- Stevens, D. (2000) *The Gothic Tradition* (Cambridge University Press)
  – A very useful introduction to the genre of Gothic aimed at sixth formers.

Film and television

1939: Wyler, W. (dir.) *Wuthering Heights*. Film

1992: Kosminsky, P. (dir.) *Emily Brontë's Wuthering Heights*. Film

1998: Skynner, D. (dir.) *Wuthering Heights*. TV

2003: Krishnamma, S. (dir.) *Wuthering Heights*. TV

2009: Giedroyc, C. (dir.) *Wuthering Heights*. TV

– These are recommended versions because of the varied approaches they take to Brontë's novel.

Song versions

'Wuthering Heights', Kate Bush (1978)

Ballet versions

1994: Muldowney, D. *The Brontës*

2005: Schönberg, C.M. *Wuthering Heights*

2009: Maric, D. *Sturmhöhe* – a trailer for this version can be viewed at: www.youtube.com/watch?v=Q3yoUbzoVVo

Opera and musical versions

1951: Herrmann, B. *Wuthering Heights*

1957: Floyd, C. *Wuthering Heights*

1993: Taylor, B. J. *Wuthering Heights*

A variety of *Wuthering Heights* opera clips can be viewed at: www.youtube.com/results?search_query=wuthering+heights+opera

Weblinks

The website of the Brontë Society and the Brontë Parsonage Museum is particularly helpful: www.Bronte.org.uk

Read up about the Byronic hero at: www.wwnorton.com/college/english/nael/romantic/topic_5/welcome.htm

Watch Juliette Binoche on YouTube as Cathy in the scene where she discusses her choice to marry Edgar with Nelly Dean: www.youtube.com/watch?v=VNmWXt-8J1U

STUDY AND REVISE
for AS/A-level

Read, **analyse** and **revise** your set texts throughout the course to achieve your very best grade, with support at every stage from expert teachers and examiners.

Your year-round course companions for English literature

Each book contains:
- In-depth analysis of the text, from characterisation and themes to form, structure and language
- Thought-provoking tasks that develop your critical skills and personal response to the text
- Critical viewpoints to extend your understanding and prepare you for higher-level study

Titles in the series:
- A Room with a View
- A Streetcar Named Desire
- AQA A Poetry Anthology
- Atonement
- King Lear
- Measure for Measure
- Othello
- Seamus Heaney: Selected Poems
- Skirrid Hill
- Tess of the D'Urbervilles
- The Duchess of Malfi
- The Great Gatsby
- The Handmaid's Tale
- The Taming of the Shrew
- The Tempest
- The Wife of Bath's Tale
- The Winter's Tale
- Top Girls
- Wuthering Heights

£8.99 each

View the full series and order online at
www.hoddereducation.co.uk/studyandrevise

HODDER EDUCATION
LEARN MORE